FOURTH YE
ASSESSMENT PA ERS IN
MATHEMATICS

J M BOND

Nelson

Paper 1

Here is a pie chart which shows how Joanna spent yesterday evening between 6 p.m. and 8 p.m.

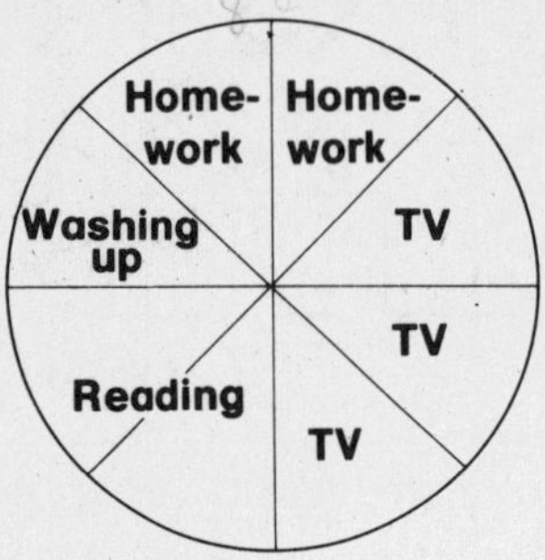

1–4 She was watching T.V. for ...., doing homework for ...., reading for .... and washing up for ....

5 £ 37·89 + 28·75

6 £ 40·04 − 17·97

7 $29\overline{)899}$

8 Make 999 twenty times as large. ....

9 $1\frac{1}{2} \times 2\frac{1}{2} =$ ....

10 $\frac{9}{10} \div \frac{27}{20} =$ ....

In each of the following lines underline the smallest number and put a ring round the largest number.

11	$\frac{5}{8}$	$\frac{3}{4}$	$\frac{7}{8}$	$\frac{1}{2}$	
12	3·07	3·7	37	3·007	0·307
13	$\frac{15}{3}$	$\frac{12}{6}$	$\frac{27}{9}$	$\frac{8}{2}$	$\frac{10}{10}$
14	0·125	$\frac{1}{2}$	0·25	$\frac{7}{8}$	0·75
15	$\frac{3}{4}$ of 12	$\frac{5}{7}$ of 14	$\frac{2}{3}$ of 9	$\frac{2}{5}$ of 10	$\frac{1}{2}$ of 16

16 Write in figures: one hundred and two thousand and twenty-one. ....

17–20 What are the first four multiples of 18? ....

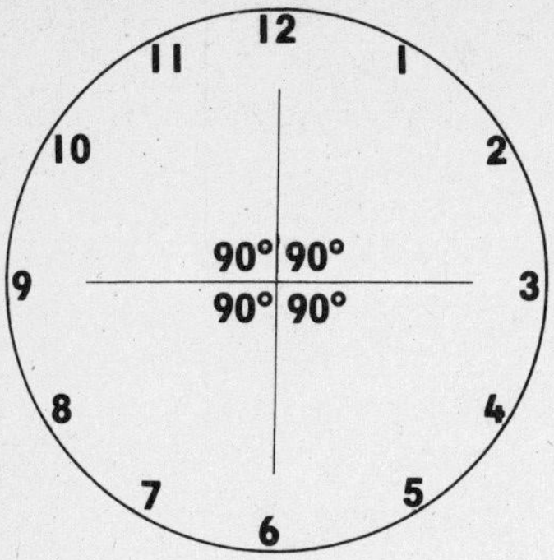

What is the size of the smaller angle:

21 between 1 and 3? .... 22 between 2 and 7? ....

23 between 7 and 11? .... 24 between 8 and 9? ....

25 between 4 and 10? ....

26 (7 × 8) + ... = 61 27 8 × (7 − ......) = 32

28 (9 × 12) − ...... = 106 29 6 × (11 − ......) = 36

Our ordinary numbers are called Arabic numbers. Turn these Roman numbers into Arabic numbers.

30 VIII = ... 31 XIV = ... 32 XVI = ... 33 IX = ...

34–35 Paul and Tim together have 84 marbles. If Tim has 18 more than Paul, Tim has .... marbles and Paul has .... marbles.

36–38 36 articles are shared among A, B and C in the ratio of 1:3:5. How many has A? .... B has .... C has ....

39 John spent $\frac{2}{3}$ of his money on a book, $\frac{1}{6}$ on sweets and he had 12p left. How much had he at first? ....

40–43 Write the set of fractions less than 1 which have a denominator of 5. ....

44 It takes me 27 minutes to walk to school. What time must I leave home if I have to be at school by 5 minutes past nine? ....

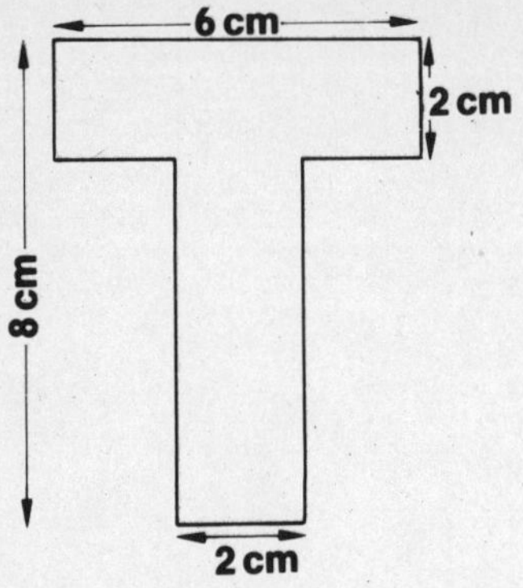

45 What is the area of this figure? .... cm²

46 What is its perimeter? .... cm

Here is a ready reckoner. Use it for finding the cost of several bottles of Squish. Each bottle costs 13p.

1 bottle	13p	8 bottles	104p
2 bottles	26p	9 bottles	117p
3 bottles	39p	10 bottles	130p
4 bottles	52p	20 bottles	260p
5 bottles	65p	30 bottles	390p
6 bottles	78p	40 bottles	520p
7 bottles	91p	50 bottles	650p

47 14 bottles will cost ....

48 22 bottles will cost ....

49 31 bottles will cost ....

50 44 bottles will cost ....

Paper 2

Divide each of these numbers by 10.

1 78·65 ....

2 6·54 ....

3 467·5 ....

4 0·123 ....

5 Find the H.C.F. of 45 and 60. ....

6 Find the L.C.M. of 28 and 42. ....

7 Find the sum of:

```
  9087
  7205
  8791
________

________
```

8 Write the answer to the last sum in words.

....

9–10 In a school 6 out of every 11 children are girls. If there are 407 children in the school there are:

.... boys and .... girls.

Here are some of Charlotte's exam marks. Can you turn them into percentages?

	Subject	Charlotte's mark	Possible mark	Percentage
11	Maths	36	40	....
12	History	17	20	....
13	English	23	25	....
14	French	48	60	....

Here are some of Peter's percentages. Write down his actual marks.

	Subject	Peter's mark	Possible mark	Percentage
15	Maths	....	40	60
16	History	....	20	90
17	English	....	25	84
18	French	....	60	85

19

```
      £
  13·78
×     6
_______

_______
```

20

```
  8010
− 1716
______

______
```

21

```
    497
×   820
_______

_______
```

There are 240 children in a school. 105 children like football, 94 children like cricket and 63 children like neither game. Enter this information in the Venn diagram.

22–24 Ch = set of children
F = set of children who like football
C = set of children who like cricket

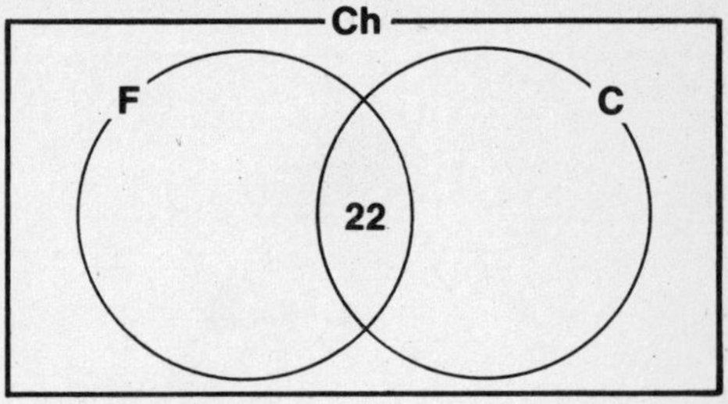

25 How many children in the school don't like football? ....

26 How many children in the school don't like cricket? ....

27 What number is midway between 18 and 42? ....

28 What number is midway between 19 and 53? ....

29 Find the area of a square whose perimeter is 12 cm. ....

Complete the following chart:

	Speed	Time taken	Distance
30	40 km/h	$1\frac{1}{2}$ hours	....
31	....	2 hours	80 km
32	60 km/h	....	90 km

Some places are ahead of our time and others are behind our time.

Austria is +1 hour — Cyprus is +2 hours

Hong Kong is +8 hours — Japan is +9 hours

When it is midday in London it is:

33 .... in Japan — 34 .... in Austria

35 .... in Cyprus — 36 .... in Hong Kong

When it is 15.00 in Japan it is:

37 .... in London — 38 .... in Hong Kong

39 $\frac{5}{8} + \frac{7}{16} =$ .... — 40 $7 - 4\frac{2}{9} =$ ....

Some marbles are shared between Tom and Matthew in the ratio of 5:4.

41 If Matthew receives 16 Tom will get ....

42 If they shared them equally Matthew would get ....

Write these fractions as decimals:

43 $4\frac{1}{2}$ .... 44 $3\frac{1}{4}$ .... 45 $7\frac{1}{10}$ .... 46 $3\frac{9}{100}$ ....

47
```
  887
  998
+ 776
-----

-----
```

48
```
  378
×   9
-----

-----
```

49
```
12)2808
```

50
```
  456
×  35
-----

-----
```

Paper 3

1
```
 kg    g
  7  360
×      3
---------

---------
```

2
```
  kg    g
   9    0
− 1  275
---------

---------
```

3
```
  kg    g
   4  675
+  3  396
---------

---------
```

4
```
 kg    g
5) 6    0
```

5–15 Complete this timetable for Merrywell School. There are five lessons each 35 minutes in length, with a "break" of 15 minutes after the third lesson.

	Begins	Ends
1st lesson	....	....
2nd lesson	....	....
3rd lesson	....	....
Break	....	11.10
4th lesson	....	....
5th lesson	....	....

16 What is the number nearest to 5000, but smaller than it, into which 38 will divide without a remainder? ....

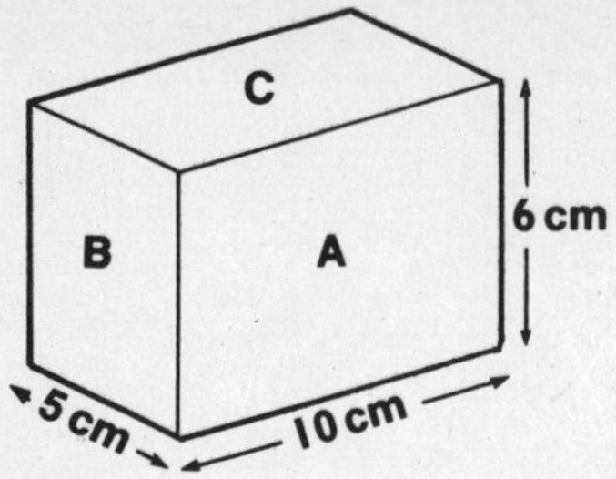

17–19 What is the area of:

side A? .... side B? .... side C? ....

20–22 What is the perimeter of:

side A? .... side B? .... side C? ....

The following sums are in Binary (Base 2). Give your answers in this base.

23
```
  101
+ 111
-----

-----
```

24
```
  1101
+  111
------

------
```

25
```
  1011
+ 1101
------

------
```

26
```
  1011
+  111
------

------
```

27–28 Alan is eleven years old and Emma is nine. They are given £4·80 to be shared between them in the ratio of their ages.

Alan will get .... Emma will get ....

29 If 11 articles cost £7·37 what would be the cost of 8 similar articles? ....

Find the area of these triangles. The area of a triangle $= \frac{1}{2}$ (base × height)
Scale: 1 square = 1 cm²

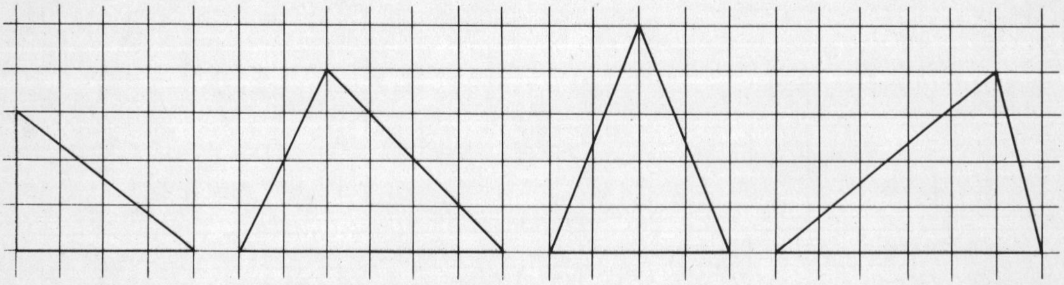

30 .... 31 .... 32 .... 33 ....

At our car park the charges are as follows:

Up to 1 hour	20p
Over 1 hour and up to 2 hours	40p
Over 2 hours and up to 3 hours	60p
Over 3 hours and up to 4 hours	80p
Over 4 hours and up to 5 hours	100p
Over 5 hours and up to 6 hours	110p
Over 6 hours and up to 7 hours	120p
Over 7 hours and up to 8 hours	130p

34 Miss Short parks her car at 12.30 p.m. and collects it at 4 p.m. How much will she have to pay? ....

35 Mrs. Rowland's car is at the car park from 9.15 a.m. to 11.30 a.m. She will be charged ....

36 Mr. Reed's car is at the car park from 2.40 p.m. to 6.30 p.m. He will have to pay ....

37 How much will Mr. Davies have to pay if his car is left at the car park from 8.45 a.m. to 4.30 p.m.? ....

VAT (Value Added Tax) is charged at 15% on some goods. This means that a £100·00 article would have a tax of £15·00 added to its cost.
Complete the table below.

	Price before VAT	VAT	Total cost
38–39	£200·00	....	....
40–41	£50·00	....	....
42–43	£10·00	....	....

44	m cm		
	4 72		
	+ 3 39		
45	m cm		
	6 2		
	− 3 8		
46	m cm		
	4 60		
	× 5		

Write correct to the nearest 100:

47 298 ....

48 347 ....

49 503 ....

50 1074 ....

Paper 4

Fill in the gaps.

1–5

	Length	Width	Perimeter
Rectangle 1	18 cm	....	40 cm
Rectangle 2	....	3 cm	30 cm
Rectangle 3	9 cm	4 cm	....
Square 1	6 cm	....	....

6 How many times can 28 be subtracted from 1316? ....

In each line put a ring round the correct answer.

7	0·1 × 0·1	= 0·2	0·02	0·01	0·1	1·1
8	10% of 40	= 8	5	80	20	4
9	10 − 9·99	= 0·9	0·01	1·00	1·1	1·9
10	0·207 ÷ 0·3	= 0·9	0·09	0·69	0·66	0·23
11	1·1 × 1·1	= 1·21	1·11	11·1	2·2	1·01
12	567 ÷ 100	= 56 700	0·567	56·7	5·67	5670

13 The product of 2 numbers is 1260. One of the numbers is 35. What is the other number? ....

Fill in the missing figures in the sums below.

14–17

```
  ...365
  2....1
+ 345...
--------
  10603
--------
```

18–20

```
  1...7...
−   2...5
---------
    786
---------
```

21

```
   345
×  ....
-------
  2415
-------
```

Find the value of x in the following equations.

22 $3x = 10 - 1$

$x =$ ....

23 $4x - x = 12$

$x =$ ....

24 $2x + x = 6$

$x =$ ....

25 $3x + x = 11 + 1$

$x =$ ....

Some children were asked which kind of films they liked. 28 liked horror films, 27 liked Westerns, and 20 liked comedies. Using this information complete the Venn diagram below.

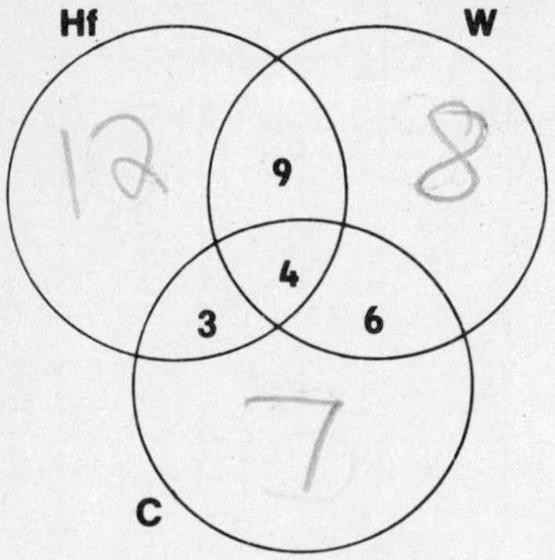

Hf = Horror films

W = Westerns

C = Comedies

26 How many like both Westerns and comedies? ....

27 How many like both horror films and comedies? ....

28 .... children like both horror films and Westerns.

29 How many children like all three types of films? ....

30 How many like Westerns but not comedies and horror films? ....

31 How many like horror films but not comedies or Westerns? ....

32 How many don't like Westerns or horror films but like comedies? ....

33 How many don't like horror films? ....

34 How many don't like comedies? ....

35 How many don't like Westerns? ....

36 How many children were asked about these films? ....

Multiply each of these numbers by 10.

37 3·77 ....

38 46·5 ....

39 0·126 ....

40 0·027 ....

41 49 ....

42 567 ....

43 0·0023 ....

Alan has half as many sweets as Brian, and Christopher has one third as many as Brian. Altogether they have 44 sweets.

44–46 Alan has ...., Brian has .... and Christopher has ....

Turn these times into a.m. or p.m. times.

47 05.05	48 12.45	49 20.02	50 15.15
....	....	....	....

Paper 5

Complete the following chart.

		Length	Width	Area
1	Rectangle 1	8 m	6 m	....
2	Rectangle 2	....	4 m	32 m²
3	Rectangle 3	4 m	....	10 m²
4	Rectangle 4	....	3·5 m	10·5 m²
5	Rectangle 5	1·5 m	1·5 m	....
6	Rectangle 6	5 m	....	6 m²
7	Rectangle 7	1·3 m	2·4 m	....

Find the area of these triangles. The area of a triangle = $\frac{1}{2}$ (base × height)
Scale: 1 square = 1 cm²

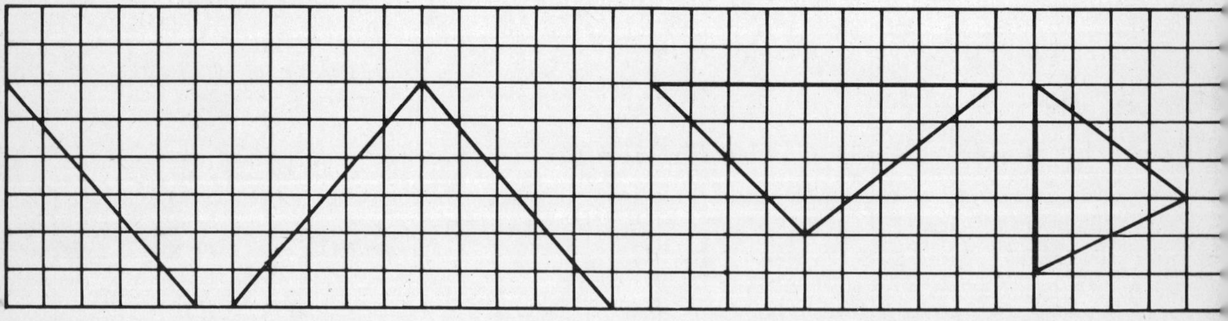

8 .... 9 .... 10 .... 11 ....

12 My watch loses a quarter of a minute every hour. If I put it right at midday, what time will my watch show at 8 p.m. that night? ....

13 I left home at 10.55 a.m. and arrived back at 5.24 p.m.
How long was I out? ....

Complete the following:

14 4^2 is to 16 as 9^2 is to ....

15 $4\frac{1}{2}$ is to $2\frac{1}{4}$ as $10\frac{1}{2}$ is to ....

16 $\frac{9}{3}$ is to 3 as $\frac{10}{2}$ is to ....

17 7 is to 42 as 9 is to ....

18 $\frac{3}{2}$ is to $1\frac{1}{2}$ as $\frac{5}{4}$ is to ....

19 $3\frac{1}{2}$ is to 3·5 as $4\frac{1}{4}$ is to ....

Reduce these prices by 10%

20 £50·00 ....   21 £110·00 ....   22 £250·00 ....

23 £40·00 ....   24 £30·00 ....   25 £280·00 ....

In an election 1140 people voted. Mr. Able and Mr. Brown together polled 675 votes, and Mr. Brown and Mrs. Khan together polled 862 votes.

26 How many votes did Mr. Brown poll? ....

27 .... people voted for Mr. Able.

28 .... voted for Mrs. Khan.

29–30 One day 10% of the children were away from school. If there were 360 children altogether, ... children were present and .... were absent.

31 A number multiplied by itself is 144. What is the number? ....

A Youth Club has 110 members. 27 of them can play the guitar, and 34 of them can play the piano. Fill in this information in two different ways in the Venn diagrams below.

32–37

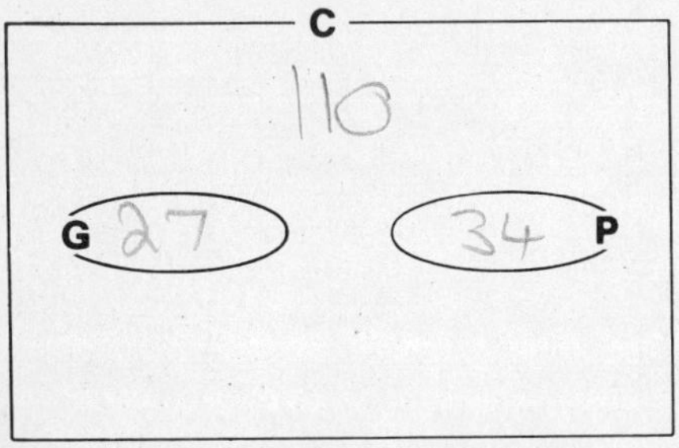

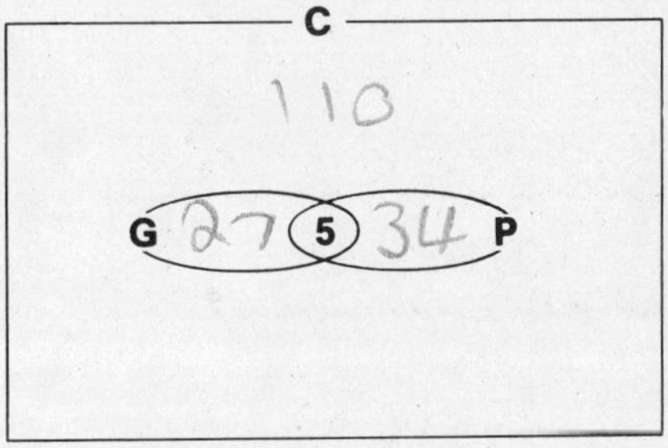

C = members of the Club G = those who play the guitar
P = those who play the piano

38 The difference between two sums of money is £1·95. If the smaller sum is £3·67, what is the larger? ....

39 A concert starts at 7.30 p.m. The first half of the programme lasts 1 hour 35 minutes, then there is an interval of 8 minutes. When does the second half of the concert begin? ....

40 A rectangular field is three times as long as it is wide. If the perimeter is 0·8 km what is the length? ....

41 What is the width? .... 42 What is the area? ....

43 I have enough tinned food to last my two dogs for 18 days. If I got another dog how long would this food last? ....

44 Add the greatest to the smallest
565 656 556 655 566 665 ....

45 What number is halfway between 37 and 111? ....

46 By how much is the product of 19 and 13 greater than their difference? ....

Gary has half as many marbles as Daniel, and David has half as many as Gary. Together they have 84 marbles.

47 How many has Gary? ....

48 How many has Daniel? ....

49 How many has David? ....

50 What is the smallest number which, when divided by 3, 4 or 5, has a remainder of 1? ....

Paper 6

1

	hr	min	sec
	3	45	36
+	5	18	28

2

	wk	day	hr
	5	2	3
−	2	5	16

3

	day	hr	min
5)	6	4	0

Here are five regular shapes – a triangle, a square, a pentagon, a hexagon and an octagon. (Regular shapes are those which have all their sides of equal length and whose angles are all equal.) Give the size of each angle formed at the centre of the shape.

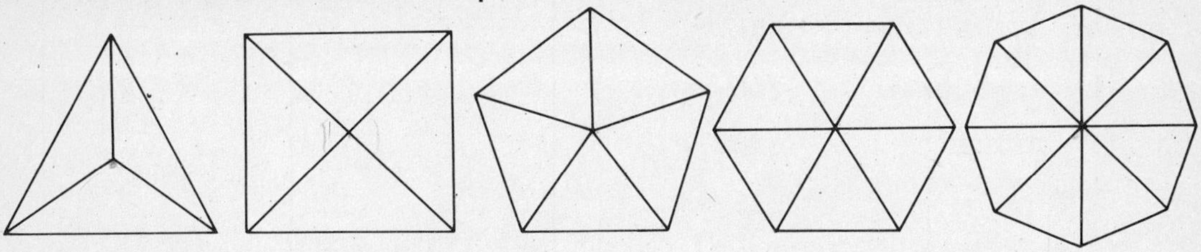

4 triangle .... **5** square .... **6** pentagon .... **7** hexagon .... **8** octagon ....

Write the following lengths as metres and centimetres:

9 245 cm .... **10** 1342 cm .... **11** 12 345 cm ....

Write the following distances as kilometres and metres:

12 1357 m .... **13** 12 986 km .... **14** 456 m ....

There are 30 children in Class 4. 60% of them are girls.

15–16 There are .... girls and .... boys.

17 Which number, when multiplied by 30, will give the same answer as 51 × 10? ....

18 Write the number which is 7 less than 2000. ....

19–34 Insert signs in each space to make each line and column work out the given answer.

3	×	3	−	2	=	7
×	■	+	■	×	■	−
6	+	4	−	5	=	5
÷	■	−	■	−	■	×
2	×	5	−	4	=	6
=	■	=	■	=	■	=
9	×	2	−	6	=	12

35 If 9 articles cost £6·30, what will be the cost of 11 similar articles? ....

Here is a list of some of the longest rivers in the world. Write the length of each river to the nearest 1000 km.

36	R. Mississippi	7889 km	....
37	R. Amazon	6357 km	....
38	R. Nile	6289 km	....
39	R. Congo	4779 km	....
40	R. Niger	4160 km	....

Value Added Tax is charged on some goods at the rate of 15%. Fill in the following chart.

	Goods valued at	VAT	Total Price
41–42	£60·00	....	....
43–44	£80·00	....	....
45–46	£120·00	....	....
47–48	£140·00	....	....
49–50	£180·00	....	....

Paper 7

Underline the correct answer in each line.

1	$0{\cdot}2 \times 0{\cdot}2$	$= 0{\cdot}4$	4	40	0·04	0·004
2	$\frac{1}{2} + \frac{1}{4}$	$= \frac{2}{6}$	$\frac{3}{4}$	$\frac{2}{4}$	$\frac{2}{8}$	$\frac{1}{8}$
3	50% of 30	= 35	20	25	130	15
4	$10 \div \frac{1}{2}$	= 20	5	$10\frac{1}{2}$	$\frac{1}{20}$	$\frac{1}{5}$
5	$5 \div 0{\cdot}5$	$= 0{\cdot}1$	0·01	100	10	0·001
6	$412 \div 4$	= 13	103	104	12	14
7	$\frac{1}{8} + \frac{1}{2}$	$= \frac{1}{16}$	$\frac{1}{10}$	$\frac{5}{8}$	$\frac{1}{2}$	$\frac{3}{8}$

8 Three buses leave the Bus Station at 7 a.m. Service A runs every 5 minutes, service B runs every 15 minutes, and service C runs every 12 minutes. At what time will all three services again start from the Bus Station at the same time? ....

Here are two Venn diagrams. Fill in the information given below in both of the diagrams.

9–14

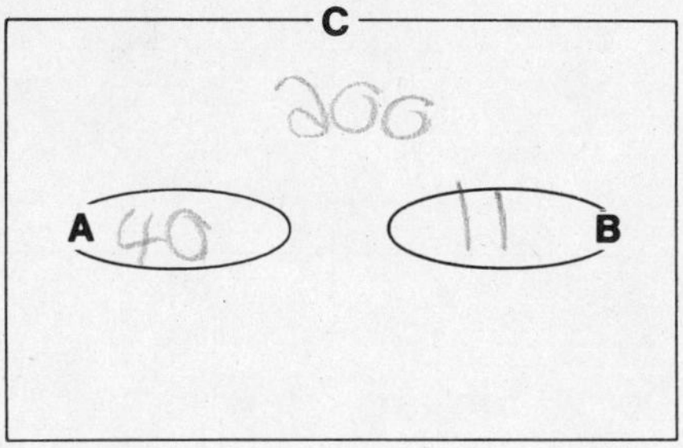

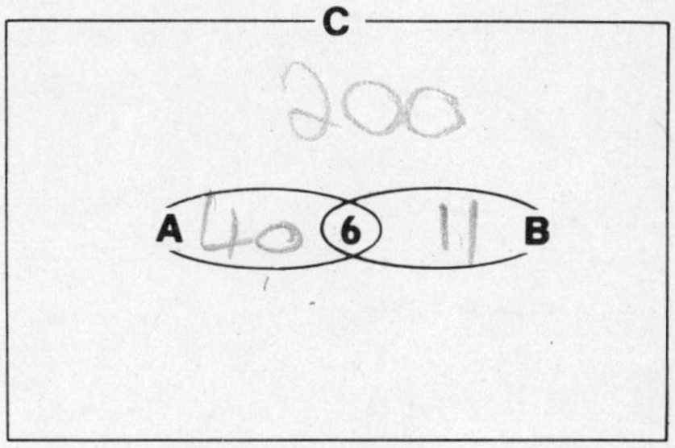

C = pupils in a school = 200 A = members of the choir = 40
B = members of the 1st Football XI = 11

15 What is the average number of: 17, 8, 0, 5, 11 and 7? ....

Andrew has half as many marbles as Stuart, who has half as many as Meena. Together they have 140 marbles.

16–18 Meena has .... marbles, Stuart has .... and Andrew ....

Here is a record of attendances of 40 children for one week of the term.

	Mon.	Tues.	Wed.	Thurs.	Fri.
Morning attendances	36	33	37	34	35
Afternoon attendances	39	36	38	36	36

19–21 What was the average: morning attendance? ....

afternoon attendance? ....

daily attendance? ....

Multiply each of the numbers below by 10.

22 37·8 ....

23 2·45 ....

24 0·047 ....

25 25·00 ....

26 $7\frac{7}{8} + 5\frac{13}{16} =$ ....

27 $7\frac{1}{5} - 3\frac{11}{15} =$ ....

28–30 What is the area of:
the flag? ....

the cross? ....

the shaded part? ....

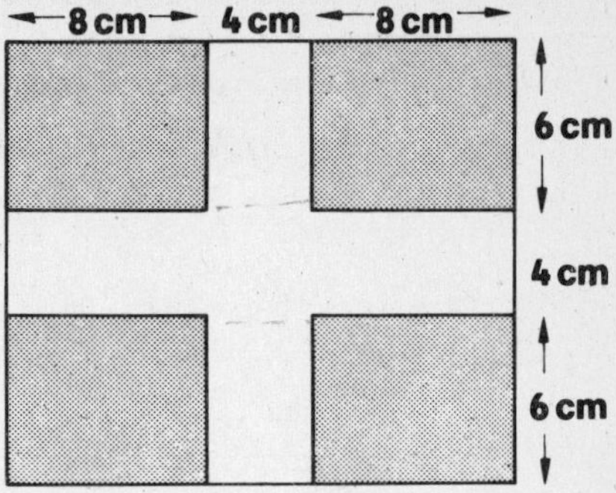

31 What is the perimeter of the flag? ....

32 What is the perimeter of the cross? ....

33
```
  795
× 407
_____

_____
```

34 $27\overline{)1593}$

35 If I travel at 60 km/h I do a journey in 10 minutes. How far do I go? ....

36 What is the difference between $\frac{1}{10}$ of 570 and $\frac{1}{3}$ of it? ....

Here is a large triangle made up of several small triangles. The top row consists of 1 triangle. In the top 2 rows there are 4 (or 2^2) triangles. In the top 3 rows there are 9 (or 3^2) triangles.

37 How many triangles are there in the 5 rows? ....

38 If there were 7 rows of triangles how many would there be? ....

39 In 11 rows there would be .... triangles

40 In 20 rows there would be .... triangles

41 Find the number nearest to 1000 which is divisible by 39. ....

Put a ring round the smallest amount below, and underline the largest amount.

42–43 13 × 5p £$\frac{7}{10}$ 37 × 2p £0·75 £$\frac{67}{100}$

44 25 telegraph posts are spaced equally along the side of a road. If there is 85 metres between each pair of posts, how long is that stretch of road? ....

45 A man's salary was £6000·00. He is given a 15% increase. What is his new salary? ....

46 A cricketer's average score for 6 innings is 12 runs. What must he score in his next innings to make his average 13? ....

47 What is the difference between 0·4 and $0{\cdot}4^2$? ....

Complete the drawings below. The dotted line is the line of symmetry.

48–50

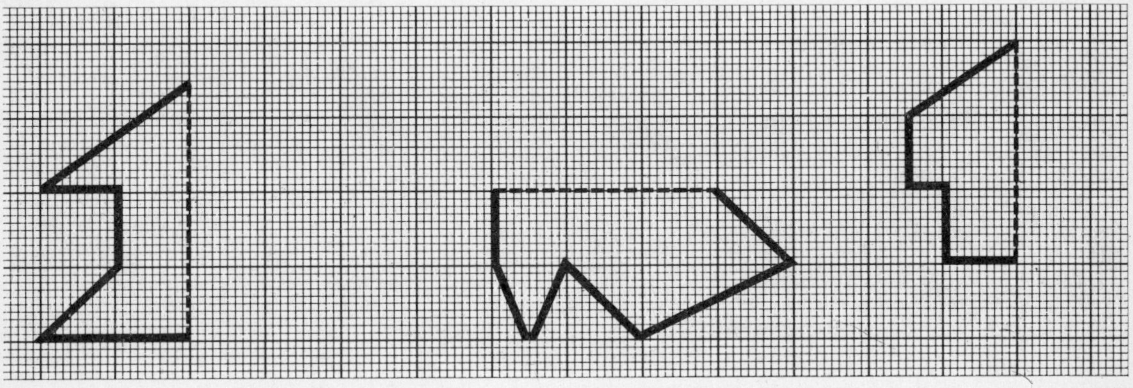

Paper 8

1 What is the difference between 0·255 tonnes and 128 kg? ....

2 Michael spends $\frac{1}{4}$ of his money on sweets, and $\frac{5}{8}$ on a book. If he had 10p left how much did he have at first? ....

3 A book has 38 lines to each page. On which page will the 1000th line appear? ....

Turn these 12-hour times into 24-hour clock times.

4 10.10 a.m. .... 5 11.20 p.m. .... 6 1.01 a.m. .... 7 7.45 p.m. ....

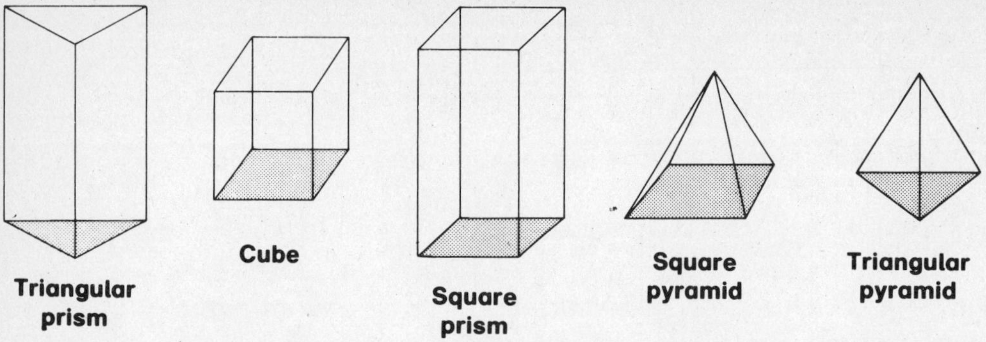

	Name of solid	Number of faces	Number of vertices or corners	Number of edges
8–10	Triangular prism			
11–13	Cube			
14–16	Square prism			
17–19	Square pyramid			
20–22	Triangular pyramid			

23 Mrs. Forgetmenot is 9 minutes late for the 9.42 a.m. train. How long will she have to wait for the next train which is due at 10.27 a.m.? ....

Local clubs took part in a "Clean the beach" campaign. Find out the percentage of members of each club which took part in this activity.

	Club	Number of members	Number who took part	Percentage
24	A	100	79	....
25	B	50	36	....
26	C	150	120	....
27	D	70	49	....
28	E	80	60	....

29 I bought 7 skeins of embroidery silk. I gave the shopkeeper £5·00 and she gave me £2·97 change. How much was each skein? ....

Complete this timetable for Workmore School. There are five lessons each 30 minutes long, with a "break" of 15 minutes after the third lesson.

		Begins	Ends
30–31	1st lesson	....	....
32–33	2nd lesson	....	....
34–35	3rd lesson	....	....
36–37	Break	....	....
38–39	4th lesson	....	....
40	5th lesson	....	12.25

Peter and Tim together have 36 marbles. Peter wins 2 from Tim, and then finds that he has 3 times as many as Tim.

41 How many did Peter have at first? ....

42 How many did Tim have at first? ....

Can you fill in the gaps, if £1·00 = 2400 Italian lire?

	Article	English money	Italian money
43	A toy	....	3600 lire
44	A beach bag	£2·00	....
45	An ornament	....	1200 lire
46	A clock	£5·50	....

47 3 whole numbers multiplied together total 2475. 2 of the numbers are 25 and 11. What is the third number? ....

There are 351 children in a school. There are 7 boys to every 6 girls.

48 How many boys are there? ....

49 How many girls are there? ....

50 A number multiplied by itself and then doubled is 242. What is the number? ....

Paper 9

Complete the following:

1 4 is to 12 as 6 is to ....

2 2^2 is to 4 as 1^2 is to ....

3 5^2 is to 25 as 11^2 is to ....

4 $\frac{7}{4}$ is to $1\frac{3}{4}$ as $\frac{9}{7}$ is to ....

5 7 is to 56 as 9 is to ....

6 Diameter is to radius as 7 is to ....

Underline the correct answer to each of the following sums:

7	$\frac{40 \times 300}{30 \times 4000} =$	$\frac{1}{100}$	$\frac{1}{10}$	1	10	100
8	$\frac{40 \times 50 \times 60}{4 \times 5 \times 600} =$	$\frac{1}{100}$	$\frac{1}{10}$	1	10	100
9	$\frac{2 \times 50 \times 60}{20 \times 5 \times 60} =$	$\frac{1}{100}$	$\frac{1}{10}$	1	10	100
10	$\frac{500 \times 600 \times 700}{70 \times 60 \times 500} =$	$\frac{1}{100}$	$\frac{1}{10}$	1	10	100

11 From the largest number which can be formed from the figures 3, 9, 7 and 2 take the smallest number. What is your answer? ....

12 How many books, each costing 35p, can be bought for £15·00? ....

13 How much money would be left over? ....

14 In a certain sum Amanda multiplied by 7 instead of dividing by 7. Her answer was 6027. What should it have been? ....

Write the next two numbers in each line.

15–16	$3\frac{1}{2}$	$4\frac{1}{4}$	$4\frac{3}{4}$	$5\frac{1}{2}$	....	....
17–18	100	90	81	73	....	....
19–20	47	52	58	65	....	....
21–22	2	5	11	20	....	....
23–24	2	4	14	16	....	....

25–26 The perimeter of a rectangular piece of paper is 48 cm. The length is 3 times the width. The length is .... and the width ....

Which members are missing from the following sets?

27 The set of square numbers less than 30
{4, 9, 16, 25} ....

28 The set of multiples of 7 between 20 and 50
{21, 35, 42, 49} ....

29 The set of triangular numbers less than 22
{1, 6, 10, 15, 21} ....

30 The set of prime numbers less than 15
{2, 3, 5, 11, 13} ....

31 Children in Class 4 have five 40 minute P.E. lessons each week. What fraction of a school week is this? (There are 25 hours in a school week.) ....

John has three times as many marbles as Keith – plus three. Together they have 35 marbles.

32–33 John has .... and Keith has ....

3 pencils and 4 ballpoint pens cost 58p.
3 pencils and 2 ballpoint pens cost 38p.

34 What is the cost of 1 pencil? ....

35 What is the cost of 1 ballpoint pen? ....

Divide each of the following numbers by 100.

36 385 ....

37 0·12 ....

38 7·8 ....

39 1234 ....

The population of Grangetown is 11 552. The men and children together number 8763, and the men and women together number 5874.

40 How many children are there? ....

41 There are .... men.

42 How many women are there? ....

43 How many minutes are there between 6.50 a.m. and 2 p.m.? ....

44

	£
	37·89
+	28·75
	______
	______

45

	£
	16·78
×	7
	______
	______

46 £

7) 128·45

47 Take twice 24 from three times 50. ....

48

	hr	min
	2	25
×		6
	______	______
	______	______

49

	day	hr
	7	17
+	8	18
	______	______
	______	______

50

	day	hr	min
3)	4	4	3

Paper 10

Look at these shapes.

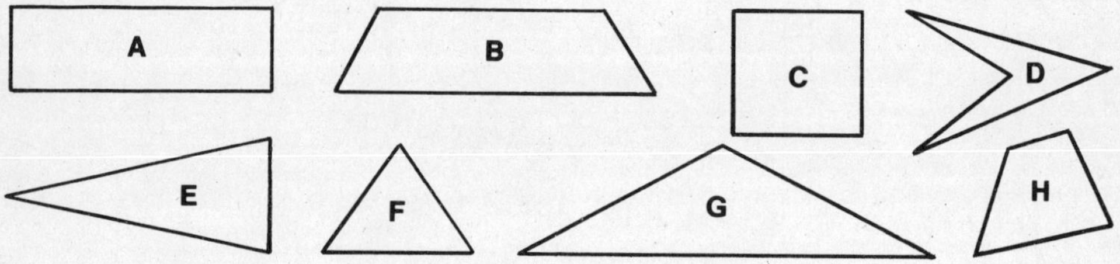

1–8 Which shapes have no line of symmetry? ....

Which shapes have one line of symmetry? ....

Which shapes have 2 lines of symmetry? ....

Which shapes have more than 2 lines of symmetry? ....

9 If 8 people can do a certain job in 5 hours, how long would it take 20 people to do the same job, working at the same speed? ....

10 What is the difference between 0·1 and $0{\cdot}1^2$? ....

11 36 posts were spaced evenly along a road 1·575 km long. What was the distance in metres between each pair of posts? ....

Complete the following chart.

	Wholesale price (Price at factory)	Retail price (Price in shop)	Profit (Money made by shopkeeper)
12	£7·85	£9·22	....
13	....	£17·10	£2·34
14	£38·75	....	£5·67
15	£17·37	£21·14	....
16	£41·85	....	£8·19
17	....	£67·76	£12·87
18	£0·87	....	£0·18

19–23 Plot the following co-ordinates on the chart and join them in the order you plot them.
(1, 1) (1, 4) (2, 3) (3, 4) (3, 1)

24 Which letter have you made? ....

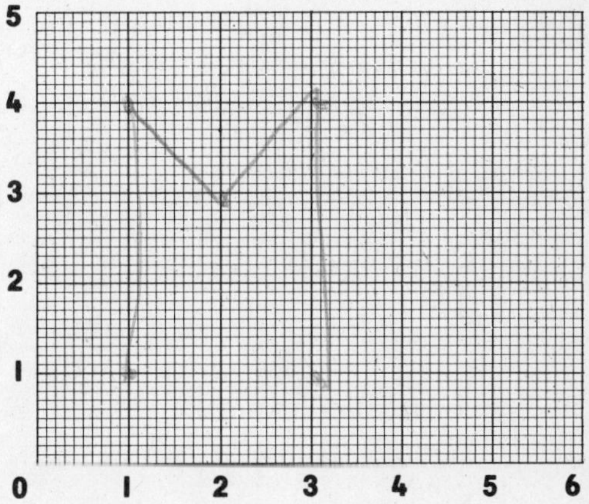

Emma, who is 8 years old, Richard who is 7, and Katie who is 5, share £10·00 in the ratio of their ages.

25–27 Emma gets ...., Richard gets .... and Katie ....

28 What must be added to 375 g to make 1 kg? ....

29 How many packets, each holding 125 g, can be filled from a case holding 3 kg? ....

Write as fractions in their lowest terms.

30 3·8 ....

31 11·4 ....

32 11·002 ....

33 3·25 ....

34 6·5 ....

35 1·12 ....

Mr. and Mrs. Black took their three children from Longford to Burbridge by train. The tickets for the five people totalled £5·39. All the children travelled at half price.

36 How much was an adult ticket? ....

	Train A	Train B	Train C	Train D
Norwich	06.15	07.33	20.48	22.10
Wroxham	06.28	07.48	20.32	21.54
Worstead	06.35	07.55	20.24	21.47
North Walsham	06.45	08.02	20.19	21.41
Gunton	06.51	08.08	20.09	21.35
Cromer	07.04	08.21	19.57	21.23

37–38 Train .... is the fastest and Train .... the slowest.

39 If I leave Wroxham on the 7.48 train, and spend the day in Cromer, leaving there on the 19.57 train, how long am I actually in Cromer? ....

40 At what time does the 20.19 train from North Walsham arrive in Norwich? ....

41 At what time does the 7.55 train from Worstead arrive in Cromer? ....

42 I live in Norwich and travel to Cromer on the 06.15 train, returning home on the 21.23 train. How long will I spend travelling that day? ....

43 At what time does the 20.09 from Gunton reach Wroxham? ....

In a sale all goods were reduced by 20%. Complete the chart below.

	Ordinary price	Sale price
44	£20·00	
45	£35·00	
46	£60·00	
47	£180·00	
48	£55·00	
49	£40·00	
50	£275·00	

Paper 11

This graph represents the journeys of a cyclist and a motorist.

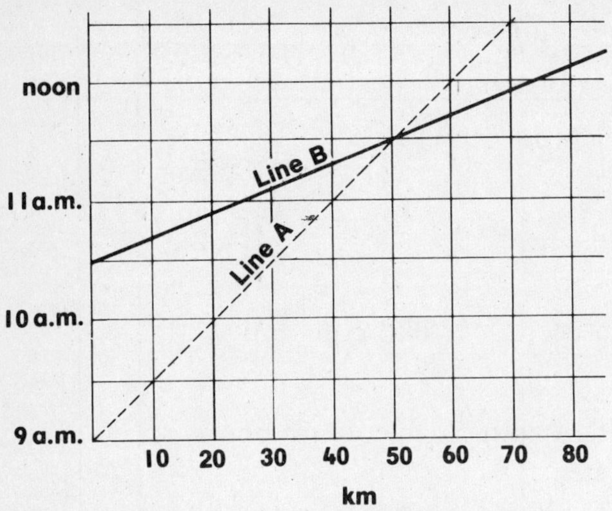

1 Which line represents the journey of the cyclist? ....

2 At what speed was the cyclist travelling? ....

3 At what speed was the motorist travelling? ....

4 At what time did the motorist start his journey? ....

5 At what time did the cyclist start? ....

6 At what time did the motorist overtake the cyclist? ....

7 How many km had the cyclist done when he was overtaken? ....

8 How many km had the cyclist done before the motorist started his journey? ....

9 What would be the approximate cost of 13 records at £4·98 each? ....

10 The average of 4 numbers is $10\frac{1}{2}$. If the average of 3 of them is 9 what is the 4th number? ....

Arrange in order of size, putting the largest first:

11–15 $\frac{1}{2}$ $\frac{2}{3}$ $\frac{5}{6}$ $\frac{3}{8}$ $\frac{3}{4}$

....

Some children in a Youth Club made this Venn diagram to show which type of music they prefer.

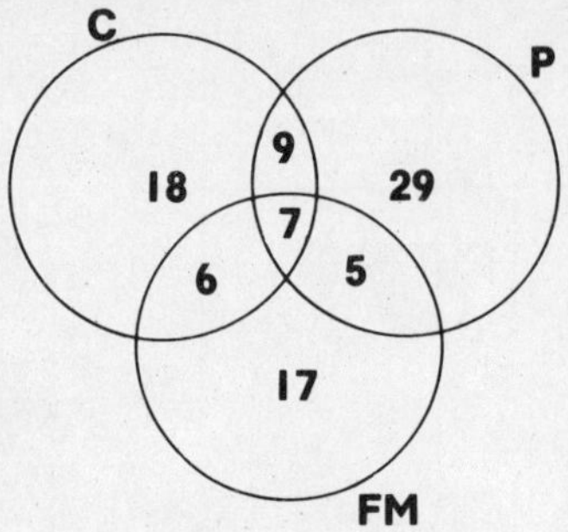

C = classical

P = pop

FM = folk music

16–18 .... children like classical music, ... like pop and .... like folk music.

19 The number of children who like both classical and pop is ....

20 How many like classical music and also folk music? ....

21 How many like both folk music and pop? ....

22 How many children like all three types of music? ....

23 How many children don't like classical music? ....

24 How many don't like pop? ....

25 How many children don't like folk music? ....

26 How many children were there altogether? ....

27 $8\frac{5}{9} + 4\frac{2}{3} =$ .... 28 $8\frac{2}{5} - 4\frac{11}{15} =$ .... 29 $1\frac{3}{4} \times 1\frac{1}{5} =$ ....

30 $29\overline{)16472}$

31 $\begin{array}{r} 708 \\ \times\ 407 \\ \hline \\ \hline \end{array}$

32 $\begin{array}{r} \text{day} \quad \text{hr} \\ 5\overline{)\ 7 \quad\ 7} \end{array}$

Underline the correct answer.

33	$\frac{1}{8} + \frac{1}{4}$	$= \frac{1}{12}$	$\frac{2}{12}$	$\frac{3}{8}$	$\frac{1}{4}$
34	2·00 − 1·77	= 0·33	0·23	3·77	1·23
35	0·3 × 0·3	= 0·09	0·6	0·06	0·33
36	3 ÷ 0·6	= 0·2	0·5	0·18	5

Fill in this chart:

		Circle 1	Circle 2	Circle 3	Circle 4
37–40	Diameter	$3\frac{1}{2}$	$4\frac{3}{4}$	5·5	$3\frac{7}{8}$
	Radius	....	....	....	....

A cash box contains some coins to the value of £5·25. There are twice as many 5p s as 2p s, and twice as many 2p s as 1p s. So there are:

41 .... 5p coins 42 .... 2p coins 43 .... 1p coins

The ages of Grandad, Uncle John and Tom add up to 104 years. Grandad is twice as old as Uncle John and Uncle John is 4 times as old as Tom.

44–46 Grandad is .... years old, Uncle John is .... and Tom is ....

Divide each of the following numbers by 100.

47 34·2 48 8·6 49 274·6 50 3

....

Paper 12

Write the members of the following sets.

1–3 Set A = prime factors of 30 { }

4–6 Set B = multiples of 3 less than 10 { }

7–10 Set C = square numbers less than 20 { }

11 Find the area of a hall which is 9 metres long and 7 metres wide. ....

12 What is the perimeter of the hall? ....

3 bananas and 5 apples cost 70p
3 bananas and 2 apples cost 46p

13 What is the cost of 1 banana? ....

14 What is the cost of 1 apple? ....

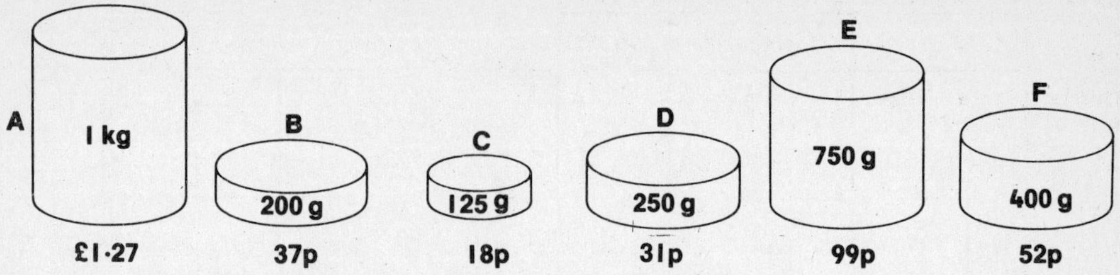

At the supermarket there were various sizes of Marvello.

15 Tin .... was the best bargain.

16 Tin .... was the second best.

17 Tin .... was the third best.

18 Tin .... was the fourth best.

19 Tin .... was the fifth best.

20 Tin .... was the most expensive way to buy Marvello.

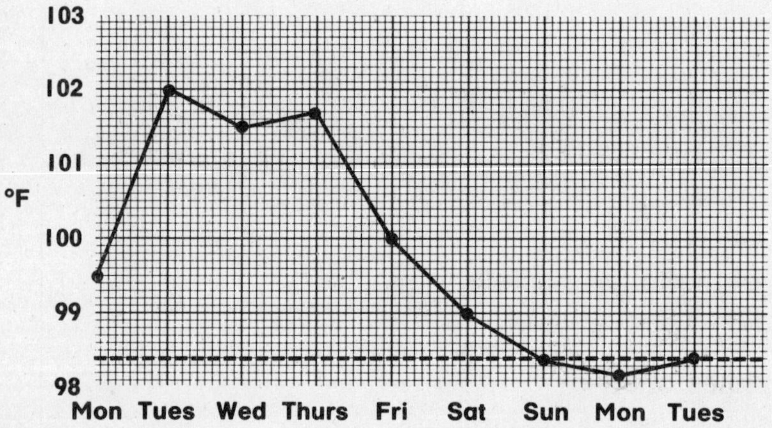

Here is Robin's temperature chart when he was ill. The dotted line shows the normal temperature of a person.

21 On how many days was his temperature above normal? ....

22 On how many days was his temperature below normal? ....

23 On which day do you think he was most ill? ....

24 On which day do you think he started getting better? ....

25 What is a person's normal temperature? ....

26–31 In the end-of-term tests Felicity got the following marks.

Mathematics $\frac{54}{75}$ English $\frac{48}{60}$ History $\frac{13\frac{1}{2}}{20}$

French $\frac{25}{40}$ Geography $\frac{19\frac{1}{2}}{25}$ Art $\frac{7\frac{1}{2}}{10}$

Her best subject was .... 2nd was ....

3rd was .... 4th was ....

5th was .... 6th was ....

Write the next two amounts in each line.

32–33	2	3	5	9	....	....	
34–35	5000	500	50	5	....	....	
36–37	1	$1\frac{1}{2}$	$2\frac{1}{2}$	3	4	....	....
38–39	0·6	0·7	0·8	0·9	....	....	
40–41	0·125	0·25	0·375	0·5	....	....	

There are 30 children in our class. We drew this Venn diagram to show how many of us belong to the Birdwatchers' Club, and how many belong to the Stamp Collectors' Club.

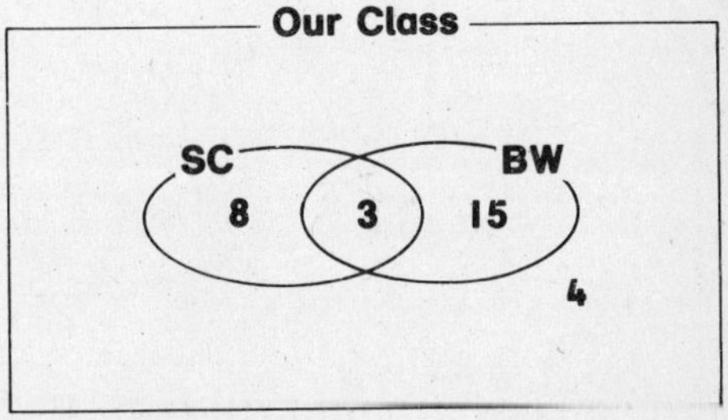

42 How many children belong to the Stamp Collectors' Club? ....

43 How many children belong to the Birdwatchers' Club? ....

44 How many belong to both Clubs? ....

45 How many children don't belong to the Stamp Collectors' Club? ....

46 How many don't belong to the Birdwatchers' Club? ....

47 How many children belong to one Club only? ....

48 How many don't belong to either of the Clubs? ....

Mum is 20 years older than Andrew, and 24 years older than Anne. The three ages total 73 years.

49 Mum is .... years

50 Andrew is .... years

Paper 13

Complete the figures below. The dotted line is the line of symmetry.

1–3

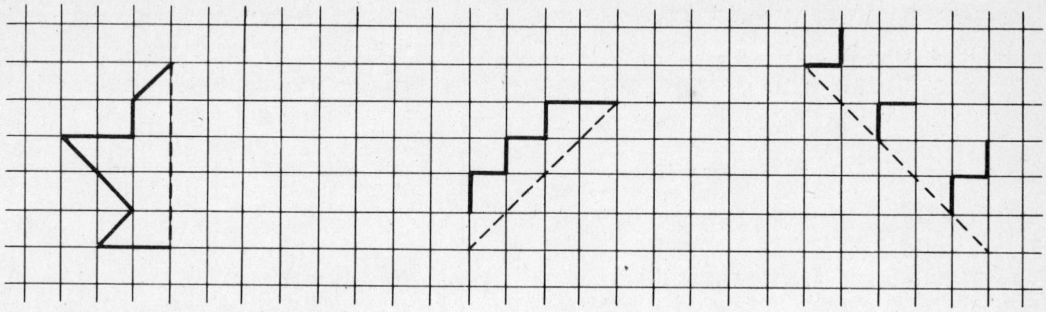

Underline the correct answer.

4	$\frac{1}{5} + \frac{2}{10}$	$= \frac{3}{15}$	$\frac{2}{5}$	$\frac{3}{10}$	$\frac{5}{10}$	$\frac{1}{5}$
5	$0{\cdot}49 \div 7$	$= 7$	0·7	0·07	70	700
6	20% of 35	$= 7$	8	20	15	25
7	$4^2 - 3^2$	$= 1$	2	3	7	9
8	$2^3 - 2^2$	$= 1$	2	3	4	5
9	25% of 1 metre	= 1 dm	1 cm	2 cm	25 cm	
10	$0{\cdot}1 \times 0{\cdot}1 \times 0{\cdot}1$	= 0·3	0·2	0·001	0·003	
11	$\frac{1}{3} + \frac{1}{6}$	$= \frac{2}{3}$	$\frac{1}{2}$	$\frac{1}{9}$	$\frac{2}{9}$	

Share £3·40 among Angela, Ben and Claire. For every 10p Angela gets, Ben gets 5p, and Claire gets 2p.

12–14 Angela gets ...., Ben gets .... and Claire ....

15 $\frac{3}{4}$ of a sum of money is £1·80. What is $\frac{1}{3}$ of it? ....

16 Multiply 3·7 by itself, and then take 3·7 from the answer. ....

17 Add together 3·7, 2·95 and 0·187 ....

18 Take 1·689 from 3·2 .... 19 Divide 799 by 17 ....

Multiply each of the numbers below by 10. Give your answers as whole numbers, or mixed numbers, the fractions to be in their lowest terms.

20 2·75 .... 21 38·2 .... 22 0·125 .... 23 0·0875 ....

This column graph shows the marks gained by some children in a test. The maximum mark was 100. One boy gained over 90 marks. $\frac{2}{5}$ of those who received between 80 and 90 marks were girls. $\frac{3}{4}$ of those who gained between 70 and 80 marks were boys. $\frac{1}{2}$ of those who got between 60 and 70 marks were girls. $\frac{1}{3}$ of those who gained between 50 and 60 marks were girls. $\frac{1}{2}$ of those who gained between 40 and 50 marks were boys.

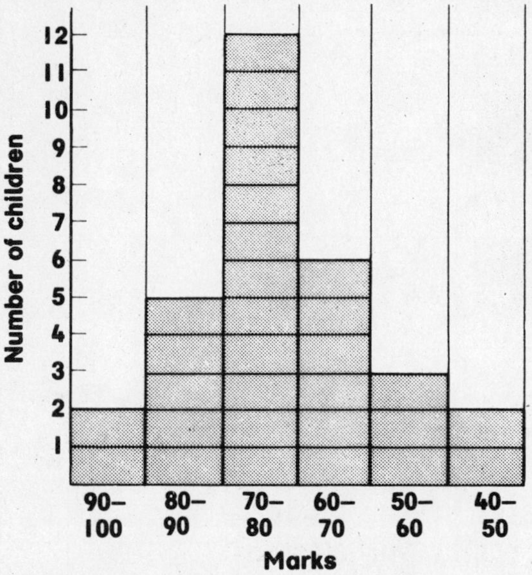

24 How many children took the test? ....

25 How many girls got over 90 marks? ....

26 How many boys received between 60 and 70 marks? ....

27 How many girls gained between 40 and 50 marks? ....

28 In the 80 to 90 mark range how many were boys? ....

29 In the 70 to 80 mark range how many girls were there? ....

30 How many boys gained between 50 and 60 marks? ....

Two friends, Alan and Barry, travel to a town which is 21 km away. Alan leaves home at 9.30 a.m. and walks there at an average speed of 6 km/h. Barry leaves home at 10.45 a.m. and cycles at an average speed of 14 km/h.

31 Who arrives at the town first? ....

32 How long does it take him to travel there? ....

33–34 Barry arrives at .... and Alan at ....

Fill in each space with a number so that each column and each row work out the given answer.

35–40

2	×	4	+	2	= 9
×		÷		+	
5	−	4	+	2	= 3
+		+		+	
2	+	4	×	2	= 12
= 12		= 5		= 5	

Fill in the missing numbers.

41 $\frac{4}{5} = \frac{\quad}{25}$ 42 $\frac{7}{11} = \frac{\quad}{121}$ 43 $\frac{4}{5} = \frac{\quad}{40}$ 44 $\frac{7}{8} = \frac{\quad}{64}$

45 $\frac{2}{7} = \frac{\quad}{42}$ 46 $\frac{3}{4} = \frac{\quad}{48}$

47 If 13 articles cost £1·56 what would 7 articles cost? ....

Share 39 sweets among Penny, Polly and Prue giving Penny 3 times as many as Polly, and Polly 3 times as many as Prue.

48–50 Penny has ...., Polly has .... and Prue has ....

Paper 14

Solve the following equations.

1 $3x - x = 18$ $x =$ ....

2 $2x + 1 = 7$ $x =$ ....

3 $3x = 7 + 2x$ $x =$ ....

4 £ 0·38 × 11

5 £ 9) 5·13

6 $\frac{9}{11} \div \frac{36}{44} =$ ....

Look at this graph and then answer these questions.

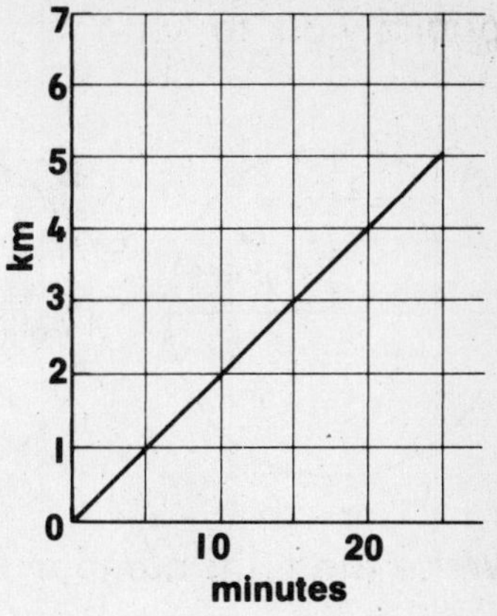

7 What is my speed in km/h? ....

8 In 25 minutes how far would I go? ....

9 I'll do 2 km in ....

10 I'll do 1 km in ....

11 What number when multiplied by 25 gives the same answer as 45 × 40? ....

Turn these Base 2 numbers into Base 10 numbers.

12 1111 .... 13 10 101 .... 14 11 000 .... 15 1100 ....

Complete the following sums:

16 .... + (7 × 6) = 47

17 .... × (11 − 5) = 54

18 (20 − 11) × .... = 72

19 (24 ÷ 3) × .... = 64

20 12 toys were bought for 59p each and sold for 75p each. What was the total profit made? ....

21 How many days are there between 4th January and 2nd March 1987? (Do not include either of the above dates.) ....

22 Find the length of a ladder which has 10 rungs, each pair 30 cm apart. There is a space of 20 cm at each end of the ladder. The total length of the ladder is ....

23 It takes me 19 minutes to walk home from school. If I leave school at 3.45 p.m. what time will I get home? ....

24 How many minutes are there from 10.29 p.m. Monday to 2.05 a.m. Tuesday? ....

4 schools in Sandville made these pie charts which show how many of their pupils walk to school.

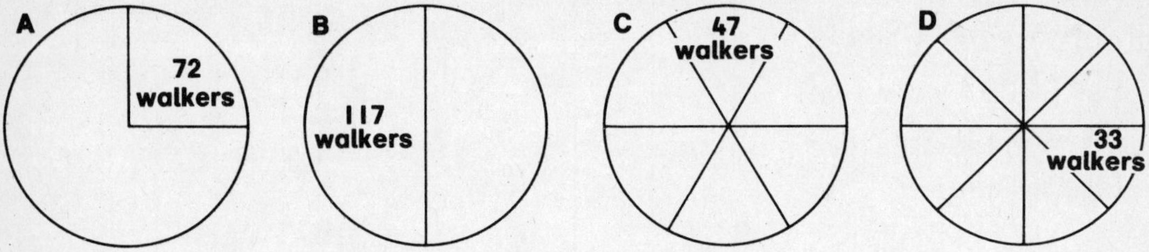

Write the total number of pupils in each school.

25 In School A ....

26 In School B ....

27 In School C ....

28 In School D ....

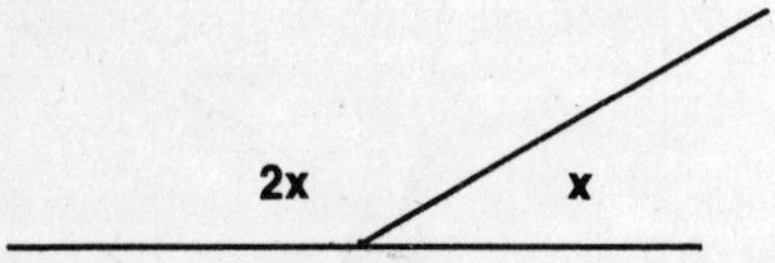

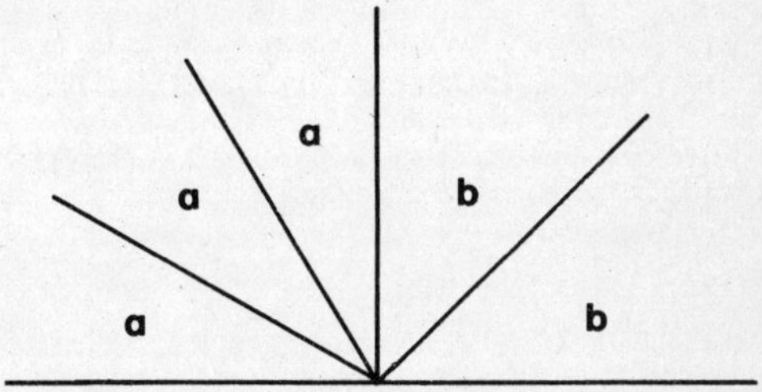

29 Angle x = ...

30 Angle 2x = ...

31 Angle a = ...

32 Angle b = ...

Complete the timetable below. There are five 40 minute lessons, with a break of 15 minutes after the 2nd lesson.

		Begins	Ends
33–43	1st lesson	9:15	9:55
	2nd lesson	9:55	10:38
	Break	10:35	10:50
	3rd lesson	10:50	11:36
	4th lesson	11:30	12:10
	5th lesson	12:10	12.50

There are 630 children in a school. There are 5 boys to every 4 girls.

44–45 There are .... boys and .... girls.

The perimeter of a rectangle is 40 cm. The length is 4 times the width.

46–47 The length is .... and the width ....

1 kg of Brightwash costs £1·20. At this price per kg:

48 For £6·00 I would get ....

49 For 30p I would get .... 50 3·5 kg would cost ....

Paper 15

Write the following fractions in decimal form.

1–3 $4\frac{1}{2}$ .... $3\frac{7}{10}$ .... $6\frac{9}{100}$ ....

4–6 $7\frac{17}{100}$ .... $9\frac{1}{1000}$ .... $11\frac{23}{100}$ ....

7 After I have bought a book costing 80p, one third of what I have left is 15p. How much did I have at first? ....

There are 24 children in our class. This diagram shows how many of us belong to the Cycling Club, and how many belong to the Swimming Club.

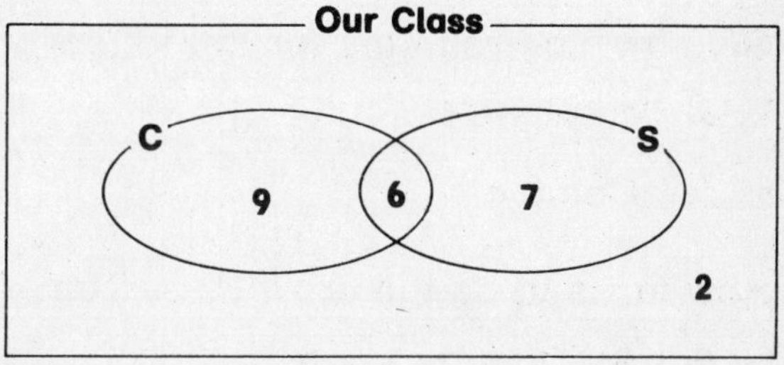

8 How many belong to the Cycling Club? ....

9 How many belong to the Swimming Club? ....

10 How many belong to both clubs? ....

11 How many belong to neither? ....

12 How many belong to one club only? ....

13 How many children don't belong to the Cycling Club? ....

14 How many don't belong to the Swimming Club? ....

This map is covered with a grid, the lines of which are numbered 0 to 6 for eastings and 0 to 6 for northings.

The position of towns is found by giving their co-ordinates e.g. Bixton is (1, 2). Some of the towns are not situated on the lines, but are inside the squares. When this is so, the co-ordinates of the bottom left-hand corner of the square are given e.g. Deepby is (2, 2).

Scale: A side of a small square represents 10 km.

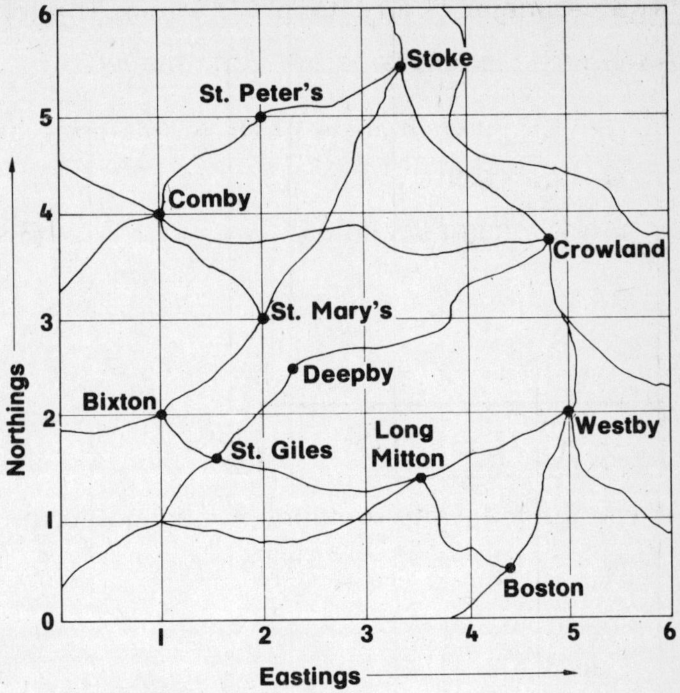

Name the towns which are at the following positions.

15 (2, 5) .... 16 (2, 3) ....

17 (3, 1) .... 18 (4, 0) ....

Give the co-ordinates for the following towns.

19–20 Crowland .... 21–22 Westby ....

23–24 Comby .... 25–26 Stoke ....

How far is it, as the crow flies, from:

27 St. Giles to Long Mitton? .... 28 St. Peter's to St. Mary's? ....

29 St. Giles to Boston? .... 30 Bixton to Westby? ....

31 Mr. Cousins arrived at the station 7 minutes after the 17.54 train had departed. How long would he have to wait for the next train at 18.30? ....

There were 364 children in a school. There were 18 more girls than boys.

32 There were .... girls. 33 There were .... boys.

34 Take 11 from 11 thousand ....

Complete the following table.

		Length	Width	Area	Perimeter
35–36	Rectangle 1	7 m	4 m	....	....
37–38	Rectangle 2	9 m	....	36 m^2	....

Write the next two numbers in each line.

39–40	2	5	11	20	32	....	....
41–42	5·7	5·8	6·0	6·3		....	....
43–44	$1\frac{1}{2}$	2	$2\frac{1}{4}$	$2\frac{3}{4}$		....	....
45–46	0·0001	0·01	1			....	....
47–48	97	86	76	67		....	....
49–50	$\frac{1}{4}$	$\frac{3}{8}$	$\frac{1}{2}$			....	....

Paper 16

Turn these 12-hour times to 24-hour clock times.

1 7.30 a.m. .... 2 9.05 a.m. .... 3 12 noon .... 4 1.08 p.m. ....

5 Find the smallest number which must be added to 890 to make it exactly divisible by 31. ....

A shop is open from 8.45 a.m. to 1 p.m., and then from 2.15 p.m. to 5.30 p.m.

6 How many hours is the shop open in one day? ....

7 How many hours would it be open in 5 days? ....

I cashed a cheque at the bank, and was given £5·00 notes which were numbered consecutively from 147768 to 147875.

8 What was the amount of the cheque? ....

Our school swimming bath, which is 50 m long and 20 m wide, has a path 10 m wide all round it.

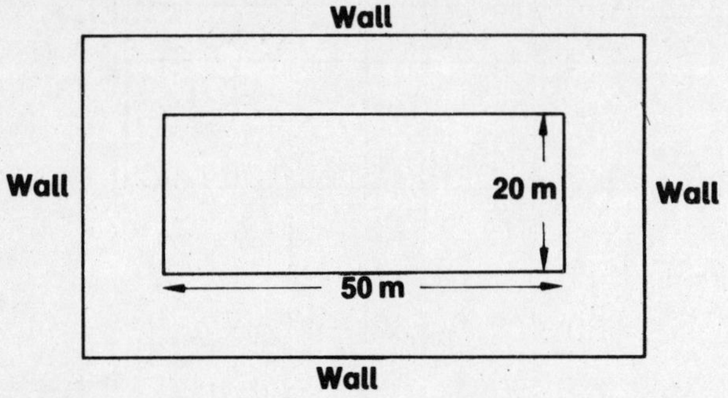

9 What is the area of the swimming bath? ....

10 What is the area of the whole complex (the bath and the path)? ....

11 What is the area of the path? ....

12 What is the perimeter of the bath? ....

13 What is the total length of the wall? ....

14 Mandy bought 7 metres of material. She gave the assistant £20·00 and received £2·57 change. What was the price of the material per metre? ....

Here is a net of a model of a room, showing the walls and the floor.

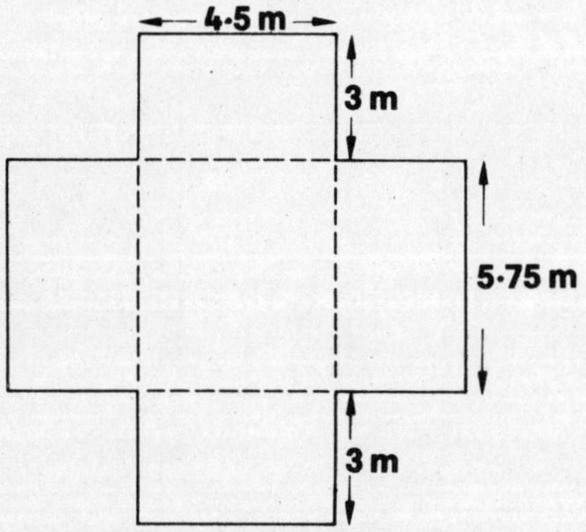

15 How high is the room? ....

16 What is the total area of the walls? ....

17 m
$$\begin{array}{r} 3 \cdot 78 \\ + 12 \cdot 29 \\ \hline \\ \hline \end{array}$$

18 kg
$$\begin{array}{r} 2 \cdot 1 \\ - 0 \cdot 375 \\ \hline \\ \hline \end{array}$$

19 km
$$\begin{array}{r} 2 \cdot 74 \\ \times \quad 11 \\ \hline \\ \hline \end{array}$$

20 kg
$$7 \overline{) 8 \cdot 323}$$

Divide each number by 100, giving the answer in decimal form.

21 34·2 .... 22 8·6 .... 23 274·6 .... 24 3 ....

Tim, Carl and Louis together had 126 marbles. Carl won 3 from Tim, and Louis lost 2 to Carl. Then they found that Tim had twice as many as Carl, and Carl had twice as many as Louis.

25–27 Tim started the game with ...., Carl with .... and Louis ....

28–30 At the end of the game Tim had ...., Carl .... and Louis ....

We asked 144 children at our school how they spent their holiday. When we got their answers we made this pie chart.

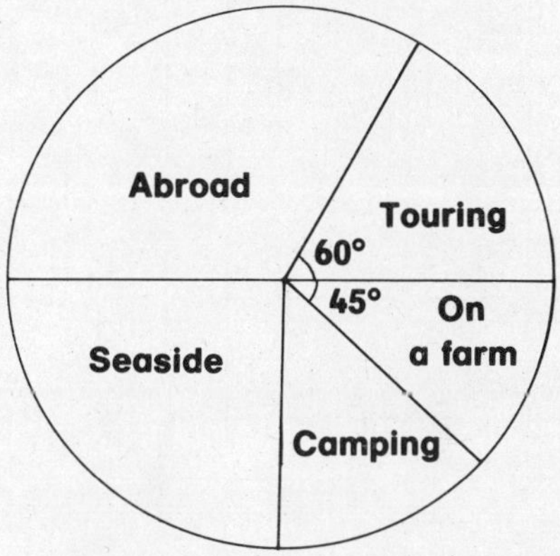

31 How many children went abroad? ....

32 How many toured? ....

33 The number of children who went to the seaside was ....

34 How many went camping? ....

35 How many went to a farm? ....

In a school there were altogether 476 pupils and teachers.

The girls + the teachers = 241 The boys + the teachers = 258

36–38 There were .... teachers, ... boys and .... girls.

Underline the correct answer in each line.

39	$\frac{1}{3} + \frac{1}{6}$	$= \frac{2}{3}$	$\frac{1}{2}$	$\frac{1}{9}$	$\frac{2}{9}$	$\frac{2}{6}$
40	$\frac{1}{5} + \frac{7}{10}$	$= \frac{8}{10}$	$\frac{8}{15}$	$\frac{6}{10}$	$\frac{9}{15}$	$\frac{9}{10}$
41	111 − 19	= 100	128	102	82	92
42	6 ÷ 1·2	= 48	5	50	0·5	5·3
43	$3^3 - 5^2$	= 8	15	3	2	1
44	60 ÷ 3	= 20	4	8	32	8
45	25% of 48	= 24	48	25	12	60
46	$\frac{1}{4} \times \frac{1}{4}$	= 1	$\frac{1}{8}$	$\frac{1}{16}$	$\frac{1}{2}$	$\frac{1}{6}$

Fill in the spaces:

		Circle 1	Circle 2	Circle 3	Circle 4
47–50	Radius	3·25 cm	4·9 cm	3·15 cm	4·68 cm
	Diameter	....	....	....	....

Paper 17

Here are Ben's exam marks. Can you turn them into percentages?

	Subject	Actual mark	Possible mark	Percentage
1	Nature Study	12	15	....
2	French	21	35	....
3	English	68	80	....
4	Art	63	70	....
5	Music	14	20	....

6 Ben's total marks were ....

7 His average percentage mark was ....

Write down Peter's actual marks.

	Subject	Actual mark	Possible mark	Percentage
8	Nature Study	....	15	60
9	French	....	35	80
10	English	....	80	55
11	Art	....	70	70
12	Music	....	20	65

13 Peter's total marks were ....

14 His average percentage mark was ....

Write each of these numbers to the nearest whole number.

15 8·35 .... 16 0·71 .... 17 4·48 .... 18 3·82 ....

Divide 1 hour into 3 parts, the 1st part being twice as long as the 2nd and the 2nd part being 3 times as long as the 3rd.

19–21 The 1st part is .... minutes, the 2nd part .... minutes and the 3rd part .... minutes.

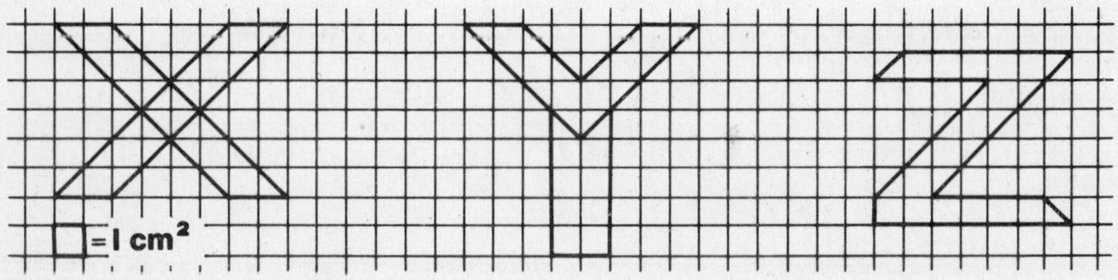

22 The area of the X is .... 23 The area of the Y is ....

24 The area of the Z is ....

25

```
  7946
  5878
  6575
+ 9876
______

______
```

26 Write the answer to the last sum in words.

....

Complete the following chart.

		Length	Width	Perimeter	Area
27–28	Rectangle 1	29 m	....	60 m	....
29–30	Rectangle 2	28 m	....	60 m	....
31–32	Rectangle 3	....	5 m	60 m	....
33–34	Rectangle 4	....	10 m	60 m	....
35–36	Rectangle 5	15 m	....	60 m	....

37 £ 15) 407·55

38 0·0907 × 0·025

This is the time on Saturday evening.

39 How long will it be before it is midnight on Saturday? ....

40 How long will it be before it is 11.10 a.m. on Sunday? ....

41 How long will it be before it is noon on Sunday? ....

42 How long will it be before it is 12.20 a.m. on Sunday? ....

Put in order, smallest first.

0·707 0·78 0·708 0·7 0·77

43–47 ....

48 3 numbers, when multiplied together, give 918. One number is 6 and another is 9. What is the 3rd number? ....

49 I spent $\frac{3}{8}$ of my money, then $\frac{1}{4}$ of it. If I had 24p left, how much had I at first? ....

50 What is the number nearest to 5000, but less than it, into which 89 will divide without remainder? ....

Paper 18

1 In a class, 19 children have dogs, and 18 children have cats. If 15 children have both dogs and cats find the smallest possible number in the class. ....

2 How many times can 27 be subtracted from 1431? ....

3 If 8 articles cost £3·92, what would be the cost of 19 similar articles? ....

Here are some exchange rates for foreign money. Fill in the gaps.

	£	Italian lire	Austrian schillings	French francs	Dutch guelders
	1·00	2400	32	10	5
4–7	10·00	....	....	....	....
8–11	5·00	....	....	....	....
12–15	50p	....	....	....	....

Arrange in order, putting the largest first:

16–19 7·8 7·088 7·88 7·008

....

Complete the following table.

	Fraction	Decimal	Percentage
20–21	$\frac{1}{2}$	....	....
22–23	....	0·25	....
24–25	$\frac{1}{5}$	....	....

Write these fractions in decimal form:

26–29 $3\frac{1}{4}$ .... $5\frac{4}{5}$ .... $7\frac{3}{4}$ .... $9\frac{2}{5}$ ....

30 The sum of two numbers is 111. The smaller number is 27. What is the larger number? ....

31 The product of two numbers is 111. The larger number is 37. What is the smaller number? ....

	Train A	Train B	Train C	Train D
Westbury	↓ 08.11	↓ 09.20	↑ 18.09	↑ 20.09
Trowbridge	08.19	09.30	17.58	20.04
Bath	08.45	09.54	17.23	19.31
Bristol	09.00	10.11	17.05	19.17

32 Which is the fastest of these trains? ....

33 How long does this train take to travel from Westbury to Bristol? ....

34 Which is the slowest of the trains? ....

35 How long does that take to do the entire journey? ....

36 If I live in Westbury, and want to be in Bath before 9 a.m., on which train must I travel? ....

37 Mrs. Gofar lives in Trowbridge and goes to Bristol to do some shopping. If she leaves on the 9.30 train and returns on the 17.05 how long does she have in Bristol? ....

38 How long does the 19.31 from Bath take to travel to Westbury? ....

39 When should the 17.23 from Bath arrive in Westbury? ....

New Zealand is 12 hours ahead of our time.

India is $5\frac{1}{2}$ hours ahead of our time.

Greece is 2 hours ahead of our time.

Kenya is 3 hours ahead of our time.

Sweden is 1 hour ahead of our time.

40 When it is 10.00 a.m. in London what time is it in New Zealand? ....

41 When it is 9.00 a.m. in London what time is it in India? ....

42 When it is 3.30 p.m. in Greece what time is it in London? ....

43 When it is 1.15 p.m. in Sweden what time is it in London? ....

44 If I made a telephone call from Kenya to India at 3.00 p.m. what time would it be in India? ....

	Years	months
Tony is	10	8
Claire is	9	6
Simon is	11	4
Mandy is	10	2
45 Add their ages		

46 What is the average age of the four children?

.... years .... months

Here is a box 20 cm long, 10 cm wide, and 8 cm high.

A ribbon is placed round the box, once lengthwise, and once round the width.

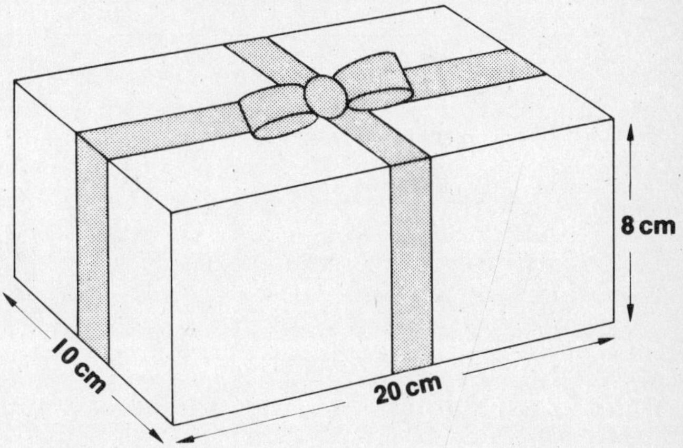

47 If I allow 35 cm for the bow, how much ribbon shall I need? ....

48 What is the perimeter of a long side? ....

49 What is the perimeter of a short side? ....

50 What is the perimeter of the base of the box? ....

Paper 19

Divide each of the numbers below by 10. Give your answers as mixed numbers, the fractions being in their lowest terms.

1 78 .... 2 475 .... 3 312·5 .... 4 1·25 ....

5 How many metres must be added to 1·35 km to make 4 km? ....

36 new library books are shared among Classes 1, 2 and 3 in the ratio of 2:3:4.

6–8 Class 1 gets .... books, Class 2 .... books and

Class 3 .... books.

The correct time is 12.43. The clocks below are all set at the wrong time. In the space write the number of minutes they are wrong, saying if they are fast or slow.

9–10 .... minutes slow / fast

11–12 .... minutes slow / fast

13–14 .... minutes slow / fast

Give the answers to the following in decimal form.

15 17 tenths ....

16 143 hundredths ....

17 47 units ....

18 7 thousandths ....

19 259 tens ....

20 14 hundreds ....

Insert signs to make the following correct.

21–23 5 ...... 5 ...... 1 = 13 2

24–26 (4 ...... 7) ...... 3 = 5 5

27

	£
	7·78
×	9

28 £ $7\overline{)12{\cdot}46}$

29

day	hr	min
5	20	40
+ 6	10	30

30 The average of 6 numbers is $4\frac{1}{2}$. If one of the numbers is 2, what is the average of the other 5 numbers? ....

VAT (Value Added Tax) is added to the price of some goods. It is charged at 15% (£15·00 on every £100·00). Complete the following table:

	Price before VAT	VAT	Total price
31–32	£300·00	....	....
33–34	£30·00	....	....
35–36	£60·00	....	....

Three rectangular pieces of card have the same area (24 cm²). Fill in the other measurements.

		Length	Width	Perimeter	Area
37–38	Piece A	8 cm	.... cm	.... cm	24 cm²
39–40	Piece B	.... cm	4 cm	.... cm	24 cm²
41–42	Piece C	12 cm	.... cm	.... cm	24 cm²

6 rubbers and 5 pencils cost £1·22
4 rubbers and 5 pencils cost 98p

43 1 rubber costs ....

44 1 pencil costs ....

Answer the questions below by writing **Yes** or **No**.
It would help you if you ruled in the diagonals.

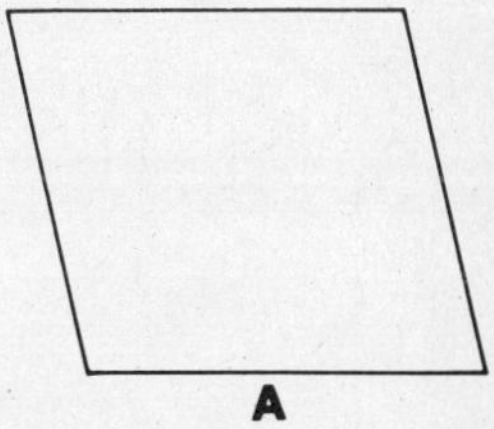

45 Are all the sides equal? ....

46 Are the opposite sides equal? ....

47 Are all the angles equal? ....

48 Are the diagonals equal? ....

49 Do the diagonals cross at right angles? ....

50 Write the set of fractions less than 1 which have a denominator of 7. ....

Paper 20

Here are diagrams of two rooms. In the centre of each room there is a carpet with a border of woodblocks round it. The border in each room is 50 cm or half a metre wide.

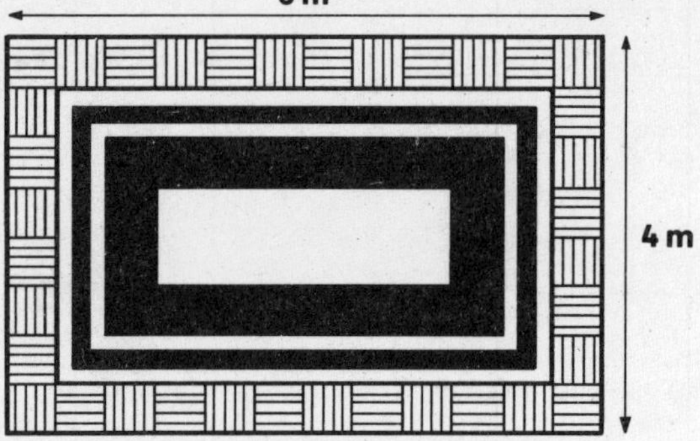

Mrs. Scott's room

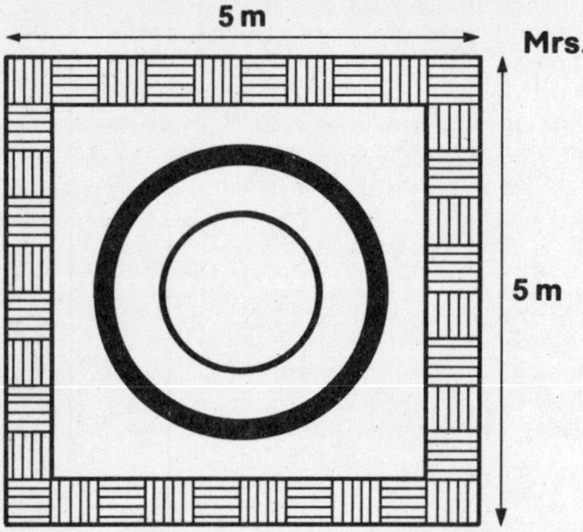

Mrs. Bailey's room

1 What is the area of Mrs. Scott's room? ....

2 What is the area of her carpet? ....

3 The area of her border is ....

4 What is the area of Mrs. Bailey's carpet? ....

5 Mrs. Scott is going to buy a fitted carpet (one to cover the entire floor). What will this cost at £11·00 a square metre? ....

6 What will it cost Mrs. Bailey to put a picture rail all round her room if the wood is 60p a metre? ....

7 In the library there were 200 books, and 58 of them were non-fiction. What percentage of the books were non-fiction? ....

In Little Marsden the population is 17 222. The men and women together number 9142, and the women and children together number 13 201.

8–10 There are .... men, ... women and .... children.

11 Take 567 from one thousand. ....

12–14 Complete the figures below. The dotted line is the line of symmetry.

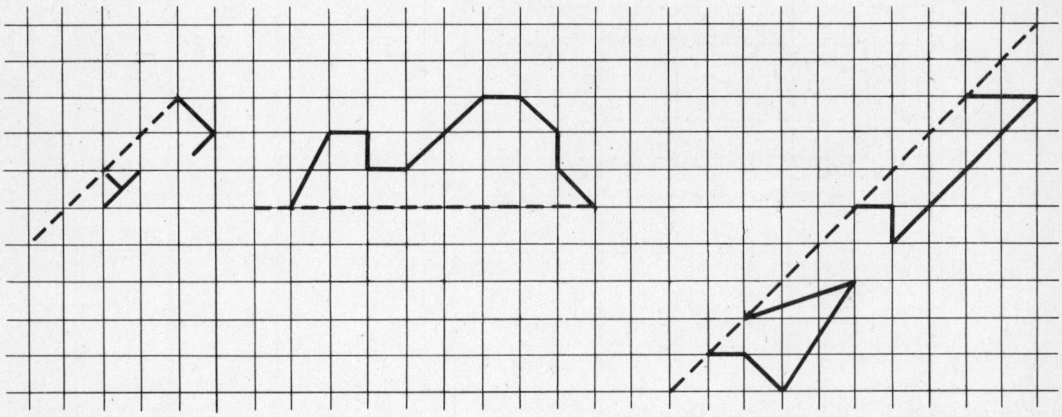

If the big hand of a clock is on 12.00, what time will it show when the angle between the two hands is:

15 180° .... **16** 30° ....

17 120° .... **18** 60° ....

19 150° .... **20** 90° ....

21 In a certain sum John multiplied by 9 instead of dividing by 9. His answer was 4131. What should it have been? ....

22 $\frac{5}{8}$ of my money is £2·50. What is $\frac{2}{5}$ of it? ....

23 What must be added to 178·5 g to make 1 kg? ....

Turn the numbers below to base ten.

24–27 10001_2 1110_2 10010_2 10100_2

....

28 Find the average of 7, 14, 19, 9 and 1. ....

29–41 Plot these points and join them in order:

(5, 1) (5, 5) (2, 3) (5, 6) (2, 5) (4, 7) (6, 11) (8, 7) (10, 5) (7, 6) (10, 3) (7, 5) (7, 1)

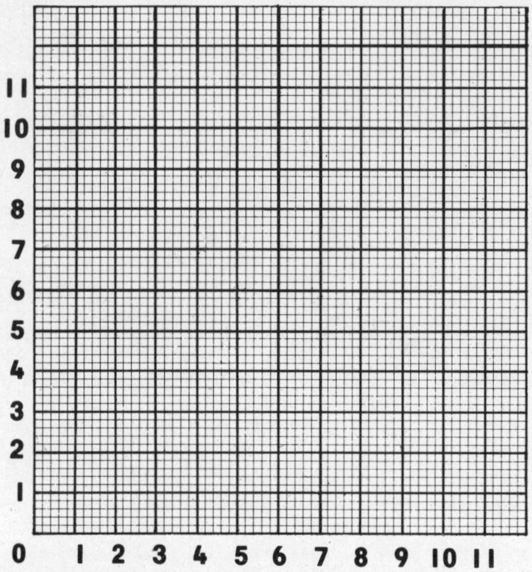

42 What have you drawn? ....

43–45 There were 227 peas in a bottle. Dad said there were $\frac{5}{12}$ of 480. Uncle Dave guessed that there were $\frac{4}{7}$ of 420, and Grandad thought there would be $\frac{3}{5}$ of 450.

.... was nearest, ... was second

and .... was third.

What will be the length of a side of the squares which have the same area as the following rectangles?

	Sides of rectangle	Side of square
46	9 cm × 4 cm	....
47	25 cm × 4 cm	....
48	16 cm × 4 cm	....

Last Friday $\frac{1}{8}$ of the children in our school were absent. There are 560 pupils altogether.

49–50 How many children were absent? .... How many were present? ....

Paper 21

At the Manor Road car park the charges were as follows:

Up to 4 hours	30p
Over 4 hours and up to 5 hours	40p
Over 5 hours and up to 6 hours	50p
Over 6 hours and up to 7 hours	60p
Over 7 hours and up to 8 hours	70p
Over 8 hours and up to 9 hours	80p
Over 9 hours and up to 10 hours	90p

1 Mr. Bond's car was in the car park from 10.45 a.m. to 5.30 p.m. How much did he have to pay? ....

2 Mrs. Green's car was there from 11.05 a.m. to 4.45 p.m. What was she charged? ....

3 Mr. Rudge's car was in the park from 9.30 a.m. to 12.20 p.m. He would have to pay ....

4 Miss Sherlock's car was in the park from 8.40 a.m. to 5.45 p.m. She was charged ....

Write the following amounts correct to the nearest £1·00.

5 £2·42 .... 6 £2·71 .... 7 £4·59 ....

8 £6·49 .... 9 £7·63 ....

10 $\frac{2}{3}$ of a sum of money is 48p. What is $\frac{5}{8}$ of it? ....

11 What is the whole amount? ....

12

day	hr
5	15
×	4

13

	hr	min
5)	6	10

14

wk	day
9	1
− 4	6

Multlply these numbers by 100.

15 47·8 .... 16 3·89 .... 17 123 ....

Divide these numbers by 100

18 374 | 19 14·8 | 20 2·55

....

There are 420 children in a school. 45% of the pupils are boys.

21 How many boys are there? ....

22 How many girls are in the school? ....

£9·00 is shared between Mick, Paddy and Jake in the ratio of 8:5:2.

23 Mick receives ....

24 Paddy receives ....

25 Jake receives ....

Arrange in order, largest first:

26–30 $\frac{7}{12}$ $\frac{3}{8}$ $\frac{3}{4}$ $\frac{11}{24}$ $\frac{5}{6}$

....

31 If 12 articles cost £15·12 what will 7 similar articles cost? ....

32 $8 - 7\frac{4}{9} =$ .... 33 $1\frac{1}{2} \times 1\frac{1}{4} =$ .... 34 $4\frac{1}{9} - 2\frac{2}{3} =$ ....

Write the following 24-hour clock times in a.m. and p.m. times.

35 20.20 | 36 08.05 | 37 00.10 | 38 17.45

....

	years	months
Anne is	10	11
Tony is	10	8
Stephen is	11	4
Sally is	10	2
Elaine is	10	8
39 Total:		

40 What is their average age? ....

We asked 72 children to name their favourite colour. We then made this pie chart.

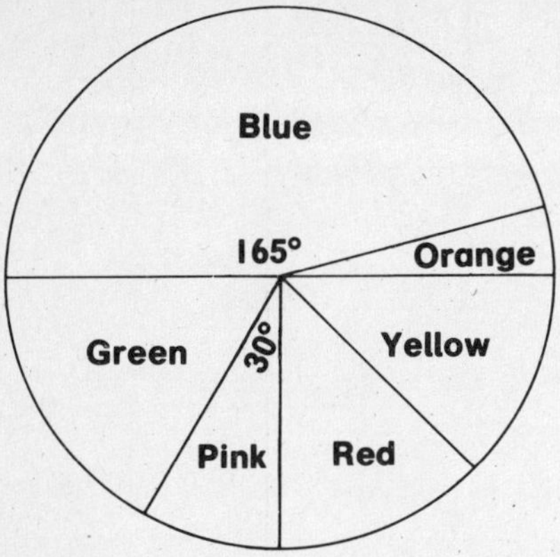

41 How many children like green best? ....

42 How many prefer blue? ....

43 How many prefer orange? ....

44 How many like red best? ....

45 The number of children who prefer pink is ....

46 How many prefer yellow? ....

Add the greatest to the smallest.

47 £$\frac{1}{2}$ £0·55 27 × 2p £$\frac{13}{25}$ £1·00 − 49p ....

Keith has $\frac{1}{3}$ as many marbles as Michael, and Michael has $\frac{1}{2}$ as many as Nicholas. Together they have 140.

48 Keith has .... 49 Michael has ....

50 Nicholas has ....

Paper 22

1 The school hall is 4 times as long as it is wide. If the perimeter is 55 metres, what is the length? ....

2 What is the width? ....

Ahmed had 30 sweets. $\frac{3}{5}$ of them were toffees and the rest were chocolates.
Ben had 40 sweets. $\frac{3}{8}$ of them were chocolates and the rest were toffees.

3 Who had the most toffees? ....

4 How many more than .... did he have? ....

5 Who had the most chocolates? ....

6 He had .... more than ....

How far can I go?
How long will it take?
What is my speed?

Complete the table below.

	Speed	Time	Distance
7–10	50 km/h	2 hrs 30 mins	.... km
	.... km/h	$3\frac{1}{2}$ hrs	140 km
	60 km/h	....	150 km
	.... km/h	20 mins	50 km

Give the value of the 7 in each of the following numbers.

11 13·78 ....

12 37·89 ....

13 378·95 ....

14
```
kg    g
  4 256
×     4
_______

_______
```

15
```
kg    g
   8  20
− 5 235
_______

_______
```

16
```
    kg    g
    _______
4 ) 5   20
```

Fill in the next two numbers in each line.

17–18	95	89	84	80	....	....
19–20	87	79	72	66	....	....
21–22	31	33	36	40	....	....
23–24	144	133	121	110	....	....
25–26	133	121	109	97	....	....

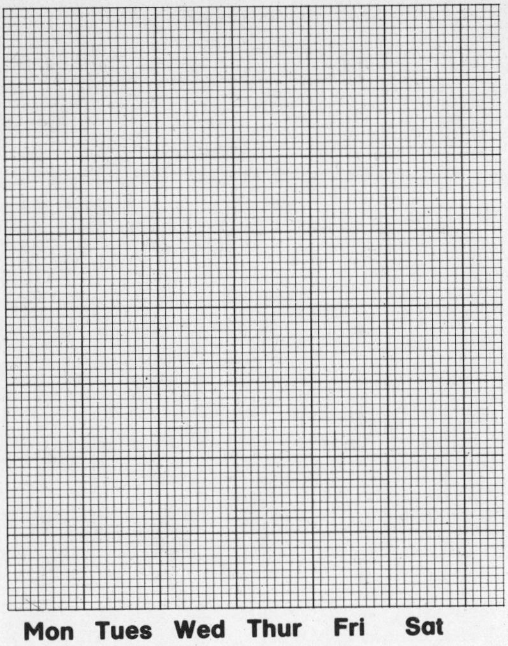

27–32 On the squared paper draw a column graph to show the following information:
The number of cups of coffee sold at Buttercup Café last week:

Monday 90
Tuesday 110
Wednesday 70
Thursday 100
Friday 120
Saturday 140

Be careful to use a scale which will show this information accurately. Write in your scale.

Here is part of a railway timetable. Fill in the times at which Train B will reach the stations. It takes exactly the same time to do the journey as Train A.

33–37

	Train A arrives at	Train B arrives at
Barwich	07.30	10.05
Hoole	07.48	....
Carby	08.02	....
Manton	08.15	....
Pemby	08.29	....
Durwich	08.54	....

At the supermarket there were various sizes of Disho.

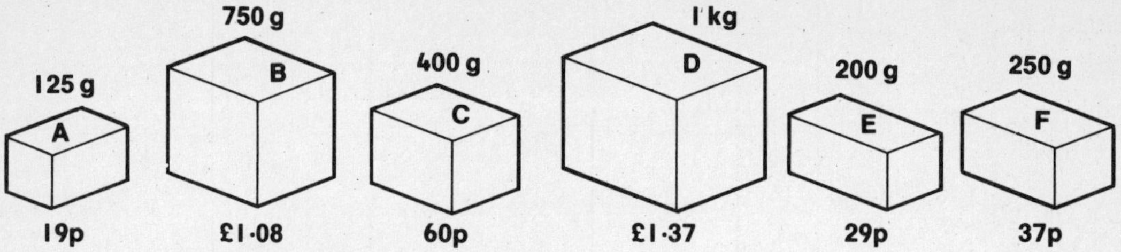

38–43 Tin .... was the best bargain.

Tin .... was second best.

Tin .... was third best.

Tin .... was fourth best.

Tin .... was fifth best.

Tin .... was the most expensive way to buy Disho.

44 A coil of rope was divided into 7 equal sections, each 17·5 metres long. If there were 3·25 metres left, how long was the rope? ....

45 Carol spent $\frac{2}{5}$ of her money on meat, and $\frac{1}{2}$ on groceries. If she had £3·45 left how much did she have at first? ....

46 A greenhouse was bought by paying a deposit of £10·50, and 12 monthly payments of £5·75. What was the total cost? ....

47 How many fifths are there in $12\frac{4}{5}$? ....

48 What is the smallest number into which 6, 8, 10 and 12 will all divide without remainder? ....

49 The houses on Union Street are all on one side, and are numbered 1, 2, 3, 4 and so on. If the house with the middle number is No. 37, how many houses are there in the street? ....

50 Cavby Wanderers had 8400 spectators to watch their game this week. Last week the attendance was 7000. What was the percentage increase this week? ....

Paper 23

A = set of all tigers
B = set of all lions
C = set of all four-legged animals
D = set of zoo animals

1–3 In each of the figures below mark the second set with either B, C or D.

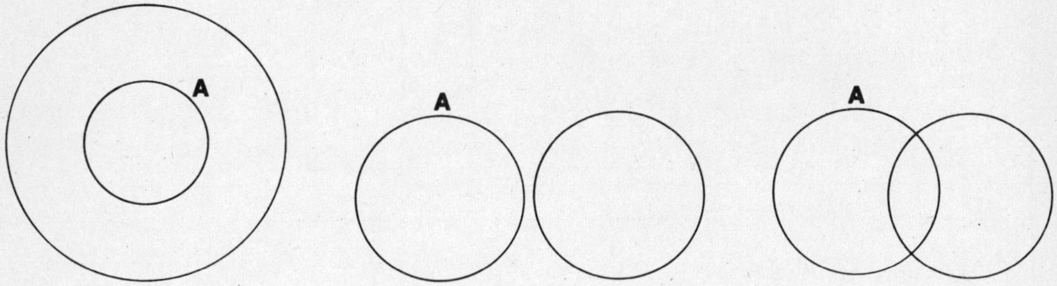

Complete the following chart. Increase all prices by 20%.

	Original price	Increased price
4	£90·00	....
5	£70·00	....
6	£110·00	....
7	£40·00	....
8	£130·00	....
9	£210·00	....
10	£170·00	....

Write the numbers below, correct to the nearest 100.

11 71 246 .... 12 1486 .... 13 1274 .... 14 704·85 ....

15 What number is half way between 98 and 144? ....

At Blackhorse Junior School there were altogether 394 teachers and children. The teachers and the boys numbered 189, and the girls and teachers together numbered 219.

16–18 There were .... teachers, ... boys and .... girls.

19 Make 478 three hundred times as large. ....

Write in the spaces the members which are missing from the following sets.

20 Prime numbers between 16 and 32 $= \{17, 19, 29, 31\}$ ....

21 Multiples of 13 between 50 and 100 $= \{52, 78, 91\}$ ....

22 Square numbers between 30 and 90 $= \{36, 49, 81\}$ ....

23 Multiples of 7 between 70 and 100 $= \{77, 84, 98\}$ ....

The following sums are in Base 2 or Binary.

24	25	26	27
111	1011	1010	1111
× 10	× 10	× 10	× 10

Find the area of these triangles.
The area of a triangle $= \frac{1}{2}$ (base × height)   1 sq = 1 cm^2

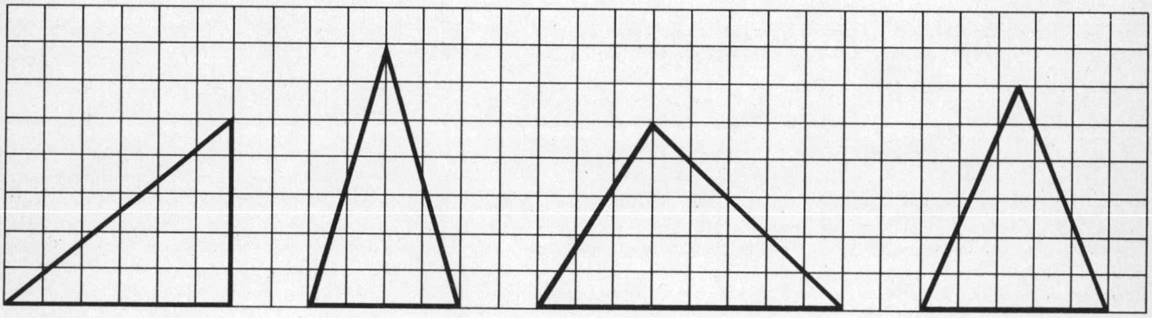

28–31 ....

Divide the year 1985 into two parts so that the second part is 4 times as long as the first part.

32 How many days are there in the shorter part? ....

33 In the longer part there are .... days.

34 If the shorter section starts on January 1st when does it end? ....

35 If $\frac{5}{12}$ of the contents of a box weigh 20 kg, what is the weight of all the contents? ....

36 What would $\frac{1}{8}$ of the contents weigh? ....

37	l	ml	38	l	ml	39	l	ml	40	l	ml
	7	850		10	5		7	350			
	+ 4	175		− 2	950		×	4		4) 8	616

41 By how much is the product of 27 and 13 greater than their sum? ....

42 There are 180 sheep in a flock. For every 9 white sheep there is 1 black sheep. How many white sheep are there? ....

43 How many black sheep? ....

44 Mr. Pin paid £7·05 for 1·5 metres of material. What was the cost per metre? ....

45 How much would 3·5 metres cost? ....

46 What is the next odd number after 160 into which 9 will divide without remainder? ....

Write these fractions in decimal form:

47 $3\frac{1}{8}$ .... 48 $4\frac{1}{20}$ .... 49 $7\frac{5}{8}$ .... 50 $9\frac{3}{40}$ ....

Paper 24

Underline the correct answer:

1	$\frac{1}{3} + \frac{1}{4}$	$= \frac{1}{7}$	$\frac{7}{12}$	$\frac{2}{7}$	$\frac{2}{12}$
2	10 − 1·99	= 9·11	8·01	11·99	9·01
3	0·04 × 0·4	= 0·016	0·16	0·08	0·0016
4	4 ÷ 0·02	= 20	2	0·2	200
5	17·89 ÷ 10	= 178·9	1789	1·789	17·89
6	2·7 × 200	= 5·4	540	54·0	0·54

7 The perimeter of a square is 28 cm. What is its area? ....

8 $\begin{array}{r} 147 \\ \times \quad 49 \\ \hline \\ \hline \end{array}$

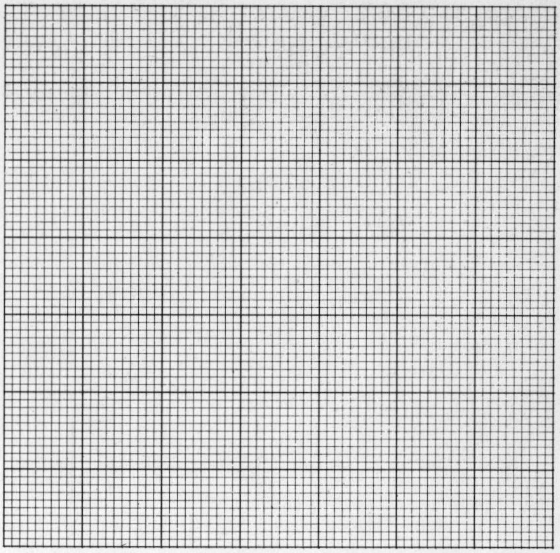

A B C D E F G

On the squared paper draw a column graph to show the following information:

9–15

Shop	A	B	C	D	E	F	G
Cameras sold	225	75	150	175	300	125	200

Be careful to use a scale which will show this information accurately. Write in your scale.

16 How many tiles, each 50 cm × 50 cm, would be needed to cover a floor 5 metres × 4 metres? ....

17 What would be the cost of these tiles if I had to pay £7·50 for 10 tiles? ....

Here are two Venn diagrams. Fill in the information given below in both diagrams.

P = pupils in a school = 300
H = pupils who have black hair = 59
E = pupils who have brown eyes = 127

18–20

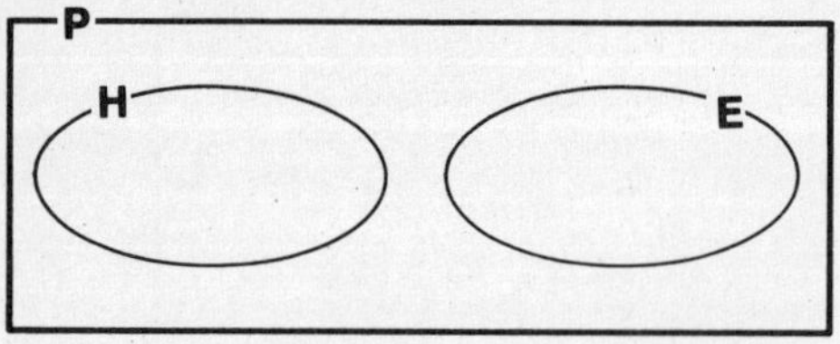

21–23

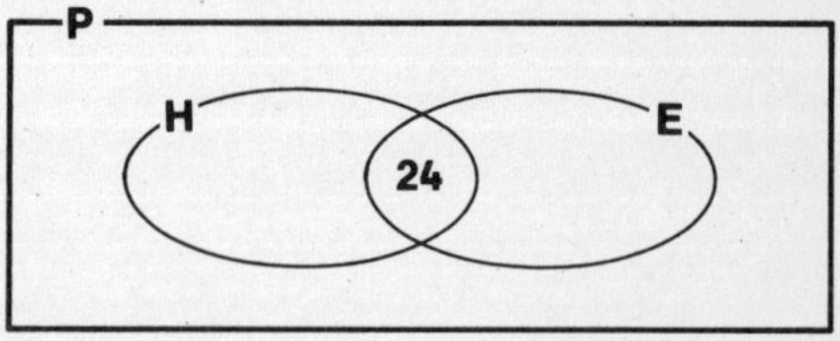

24 How many times can 34 be subtracted from 986? ....

25 Ted has 98p and Tom has 64p. How much must Ted give Tom so that they will each have the same amount? ....

There are 550 children in our school. Next term the buildings are being enlarged and we will have 10% more pupils.

26 How many children will there be next term? ....

3 numbers, A, B and C multiplied together equal 1944.
A × B = 216 and A × C = 162.

27–29 A is ...., B is .... and C is ....

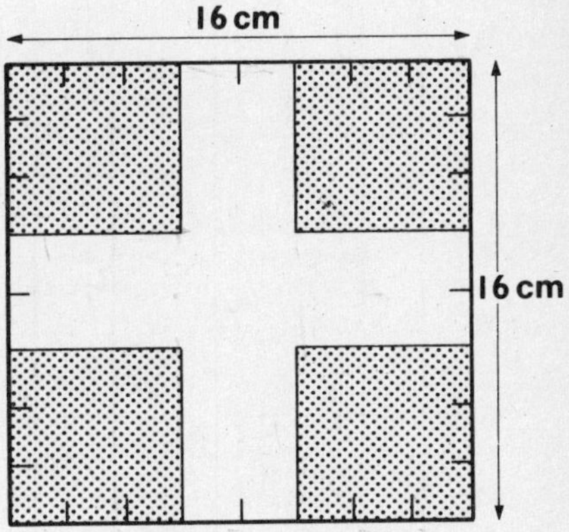

30 The area of the flag is ....

31 The area of the cross is ....

32 The shaded part has an area of ....

33 The perimeter of the flag is ....

34 The perimeter of the cross is ....

Complete the following:

	Fraction	Decimal	Percentage
35–36	$\frac{3}{10}$	....	....
37–38	$\frac{7}{100}$	....	....
39–40	....	0·25	....
41–42	$\frac{1}{20}$	....	....

43 8 − 1·127 ....

44 7·625 ÷ 2·5 ....

Complete the following table.

	Wholesale price	Retail price	Profit
45	£18·75	£23·50	....
46	....	£70·20	£11·35
47	£5·13	....	97p
48	£196·50	£235·25	....
49	....	£13·50	£2·19
50	93p	....	19p

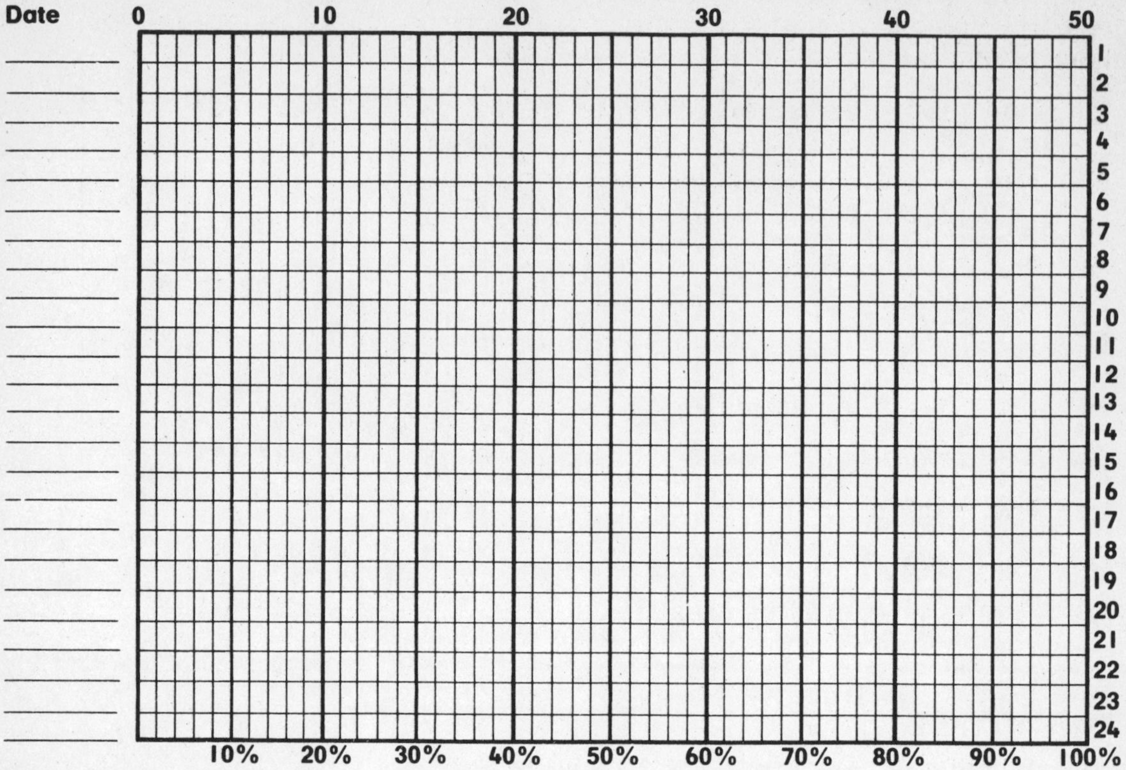

Thomas Nelson and Sons Ltd
Nelson House Mayfield Road
Walton-on-Thames Surrey KT12 5PL UK

51 York Place
Edinburgh EH1 3JD UK

Thomas Nelson (Hong Kong) Ltd
Toppan Building 10/F 22A Westlands Road
Quarry Bay Hong Kong

Thomas Nelson Australia
102 Dodds Street South Melbourne
Victoria 3205 Australia

Nelson Canada
1120 Birchmount Road Scarborough
Ontario M1K 5G4 Canada

First published by Thomas Nelson and Sons Ltd 1977
Second edition 1983
Revised edition 1986

Pupil's Book ISBN 0-17-424454-1
NPN 10 9
Answer Book ISBN 0-17-424458-4
NPN 20 19 18 17 16 15 14 13 12

By the same author
Introductory, First, Second and Third Year Assessment Papers in Mathematics

Introductory, First, Second, Third and Fourth Year Assessment Papers in English

First, Second, Third and Fourth Year Assessment Papers in Reasoning

Filmset in the Nelson Teaching Alphabet
by Mould Type Foundry Ltd
Dunkirk Lane Leyland England

Printed in England
by Ebenezer Baylis & Son Ltd
The Trinity Press Worcester and London